Ruby is a talented writer with wonderful instincts and interpretations. Her work is a fine read with amazing memories. I pray that this book will be a blessing and inspiration to everyone who reads it.

—Pastor Don Haywood,
Living Waters Victory Church

An insightful way of looking at everyday events and activities in God's creation and turning them into powerful life lessons. Ruby encourages readers to let go of the struggles and storms of life and allow them to become the motivation to overcome obstacles and setbacks, turning them into opportunities for spiritual growth. Very inspiring and well written.

—Dr. Ron Leech,
Honorary Apostolic Leader of Ministers Fellowship International

Meri,
Thanks so much for everything.
I'm glad you're my guy,
see you at the party!
Ruby Wiebe

ON THE WAY TO THE

101 Inspirations to Get You There

Ruby (Heppner) Wiebe

ON THE WAY TO THE PARTY
Copyright © 2020 by Ruby (Heppner) Wiebe

Unless otherwise indicated, scripture quotations are taken from the New King James Version®. Copyright © 1982 by Thomas Nelson, Inc. Used by permission. All rights reserved. • Scripture quotations marked (NIV) are taken from the Holy Bible, NEW INTERNATIONAL VERSION®, NIV® Copyright © 1973, 1978, 1984, 2011 by Biblica, Inc.® Used by permission. All rights reserved worldwide. • Scripture quotations marked (NLT) are taken from the Holy Bible, New Living Translation, copyright ©1996, 2004, 2007 by Tyndale House Foundation. Used by permission of Tyndale House Publishers, Inc., Carol Stream, Illinois 60188. All rights reserved. • Scripture quotations marked (TLB) are taken from The Living Bible copyright © 1971 by Tyndale House Foundation. Used by permission of Tyndale House Publishers Inc., Carol Stream, Illinois 60188. All rights reserved. The Living Bible, TLB, and the The Living Bible logo are registered trademarks of Tyndale House Publishers. • Scripture quotations marked (NASB) are taken from the New American Standard Bible®, Copyright © 1960, 1962, 1963, 1968, 1971, 1972, 1973, 1975, 1977, 1995 by The Lockman Foundation. Used by permission.

Printed in Canada

ISBN: 978-1-4866-1992-4
eBook ISBN: 978-1-4866-1993-1

Word Alive Press
119 De Baets Street Winnipeg, MB R2J 3R9
www.wordalivepress.ca

Cataloguing in Publication information can be obtained from Library and Archives Canada.

To my late husband, Larry Heppner, whose love of people and celebration was the inspiration behind this work.

To my children and grandchildren, who will continue the legacy.

Acknowledgements

All my blog followers:
Your encouragement kept me going from week to week.

Word Alive Press:
Thank you for all your help and guidance.

My husband, Larry:
I couldn't have done it without your belief in me and your
technical support every step of the way.

Introduction

Consider your life for a moment. So much gets packed into the few short years we're given to journey this earth. Our eternal celebration in the presence of our Lord and Saviour, Jesus Christ, and all those we love, is simply the culmination of all that has gone before.

In this book I share with you some of the joys and challenges of my own life, as well as little lessons learned along the way. I hope and pray that it will serve to inspire you, the reader, to continue faithfully on the path God has prepared for you.

I have broken the book into bite-sized pieces that are easy to swallow and digest, giving you the strength and promise you need to go on your way!

Remember, it's not what happens that will determine if you win or lose this "race." It's how you respond that will be cause for concern or celebration.

Everyone loves a party, but we don't all enjoy the drive over. A lot of things can happen on the way—sad things, happy things, crazy things—and they all affect us differently, depending on how we respond. Consider this your personal invitation to join me. Grab a coffee and let me share a few things with you, things I've experienced on this journey. It's another day to celebrate and enjoy the journey on the way to the party, that day when we ultimately begin our eternal homecoming celebration in the presence of our Lord and Saviour!

Choose to enjoy the journey and be inspired!

On the Way to the Party

In the Old Testament, God often admonished parents and grandparents to teach the younger generation and remind them of His goodness and faithfulness over the years. Why? To keep them mindful of His acts on their behalf. Monuments were built and feasts were established—and I'm talking about FEASTS! Many of them lasted for at least a week. These people knew how to P-A-R-T-Y!

My late husband was a big believer in celebrating. We celebrated and told our children many stories of our early days as a family. We pointed out how God led us together and how He provided for us in many different situations. We shared all the blessings He showered on us— things that are so easy to take for granted. Our kids were able to share in many of those blessings as well.

Larry, my first husband, has now arrived at the ultimate celebration; he's at the party!

When I refer to being in the presence of Jesus as a party, I'm not being flippant. Think about this: When are you happiest? When is joy most evident? When do you feel the best, on top of the world? I venture to say it's when you're surrounded by family, friends, and/or other people who are also experiencing the most amazing time of their lives. Sounds like a party to me!

We're all on a path to somewhere. I would much rather be on my way to a party than headed toward an accident scene. Every day things happen in our lives that we can allow to go over our heads, not even giving them a thought, *or* we can learn a lesson and be encouraged and challenged by them. Maybe we can simply enjoy reflecting on what happened today.

When things happen as I walk through my day, I try to keep my mind and heart open for God to speak to me. And you know what? He does! Insignificant things really, but with significant impact when tuned in to my Lord! I'd love to share some of these fun, crazy little things that leave me enjoying life to the full. I'm loving the journey and would really love to have you join me on the way to the party!

On the Way to the Party
I CHANGED MY MIND

Years ago, when my oldest daughter was only three, I took her with me to a pre-natal doctor's visit. In those days in our small town, it was common for the receptionist to keep an eye on little ones in the waiting room. Moms, don't try that today! To make the wait easier, I had bought her a small treat she could enjoy while waiting for me. She proudly clutched her choice of goodies (bubble gum, no less) in her chubby little hand as she informed me that she would save three pieces for her brother. I encouraged her in this endeavour of generosity.

On my return to the waiting room a little later, I noticed that her hands were empty and her already-chubby cheeks were bulged out quite to their limits! After a quick pocket check, I asked, "Where are the pieces you saved for Scottie?"

Her answer? "I (chomp, chomp) changed my mind (chomp, chomp)." Her reply came without the slightest trace of remorse! As funny as it seemed and as much as I laughed later as I related the incident to her dad, it certainly got me thinking.

In 1 Timothy 6:17b, Paul charges us not to trust in the uncertainty of riches but in *"God, who gives us richly all things to enjoy."* He generously gives us all we need to bring real joy into our lives. In Jeremiah 29:11,

He promises that He knows what He has planned for me; His plans are to prosper me and not to harm me, to give me hope and a future.

He gives generously all we need for a life filled with joy and purpose. Our heavenly Father has promised to give to us abundantly, and God, we can be sure, will *never* change His mind! His promises keep me strong and filled with anticipation as I continue on my way to the party.

On the Way to the Party
"IF YOU HAD BEEN HERE …"

I often hear of many families dealing with sick children: flus, colds, and infections of various kinds. It takes me back to a time that seems like yesterday. One day our oldest daughter was so ill, we needed a doctor to come to the house. After a rather thorough examination, he determined it was probably a case of strep throat. During the night, our son woke us, complaining of a headache, a sore throat, and an upset tummy. As if one sick child wasn't enough!

"Oh no," I groaned as I went about collecting all the "nursing" necessities. That still wasn't enough. No sooner had I drifted off again when I was awakened, this time by the whimpering of our one-year old baby. While changing her, I noticed she was burning up with fever, also having developed a cough and runny nose in a few short hours. Before I left her room, I turned to the single bed next to the crib and felt the forehead and cheeks of our four-year-old daughter.

This can't be, I thought. *I'm just paranoid.*

But it was! Morning finally came and with it four sick children. The two oldest stayed home from school. The little girls played and napped intermittently, and I was kept busy running for juice, ginger ale, Tylenol, Kleenex, and clean diapers. Breathless by evening, I flopped into a chair and thought, like Martha of Bethany, "Lord, if you had been here, this wouldn't be happening!"

Very gently I heard the voice of my Lord. "I am with you always, even to the end of the age." Well, it certainly felt like the end to me! I had to admit, though, He'd been there for me all day long. There had been enough emotional stamina to take me from one crisis to the next, enough physical health and strength to keep me on my feet all day long. But oh, I did long for my husband's homecoming, just to give me a little break with the kids!

And there he was! The door opened as the thought surfaced. Shuffling into the kitchen, he looked at me with weary eyes. In a hoarse voice, he spoke. "Oh, my throat and my head ... I feel awful."

"Lord, are you still here?"

The answer came quickly and quietly. "As your days, so will your strength be!"

"Thank you, Lord."

And every day I draw strength from that promise as I encounter all kinds of challenges on my way to the party!

On the Way to the Party
SOMETIMES I FEEL LIKE MY WASHER

Yes, there are days when I feel that if another load is added, I may not survive! Come on, I know you've been there!

"Please, Lord," I whispered as I dumped the first load of the day's laundry into my old washer. "Please keep it going for a few more loads."

Hey, I thought to myself, *this is becoming a habit*. The old machine was making funny noises again, and I did not want to pay another repair bill. So I prayed as it sluggishly began to move the clothes around and do its job. It just kept going, one load at a time, one load after another.

You know, some days I feel just like that old washer! I feel like I can't bear one more load being dumped on me. I moan, groan, and grind my way through the day. Every so often, my Master has to come and balance my load. I tend to start jumping around and making a lot of unnecessary noises when I get "unbalanced!"

Yes, sometimes I just need to talk to my friend Jesus and tell Him exactly what I'm feeling. He then gives me a promise found in Matthew 11:28–30, inviting me to come to Him so that He can take my burdens and give me rest. He lightens the load and keeps me going, one load at a time, and one step at a time, as I continue my journey on the way to the party!

On the Way to the Party
I NEED AN REST

As we approach Christmas and the busyness it brings, we look at the season in one of several ways. Our perspective depends so much on our basic personality type, where we are in life, and on the circumstances in which we find ourselves at that moment.

When our children were young, I looked forward to going out to one activity or another every night for the two weeks preceding Christmas Day. With four little ones, we were ensured plenty of things to do during this time. Of course, there was the big kick-off with tree decorating night, which always ended with sampling the first bit of Christmas baking! There were school concerts, church concerts, and, of course, the rehearsals in preparation. Choir concerts with siblings' participation had to be attended, and there was always a date with Santa at the mall (until the kids decided they were too old for that "baby stuff").

One of my favourite activities was taking an evening drive to view all the beautiful decorations on others' yards, stashing away a few ideas to incorporate next year. One time we drove clear across the city to take the kids on a train ride. A home owner had set it up so that families could come and sit in the open air on his mini train cars. So there we sat, freezing our butts, fingers, and toes as we rode along and enjoyed a lovely view of the woods around the fully-decorated and lit up acreage. It must have been around -30 degrees Celsius out there! A bit of a fun spoiler, but we did it—and the hot cocoa at the end was much appreciated!

These days I prefer to keep my recliner from drifting off the floor, enjoying the warmth of my fire as I read and listen to inspirational Christmas music, or simply watch a Christmas movie. After a busy day of whatever needs to be done, I like to reflect on and remember what Christmas is all about. Don't get me wrong, I love all the trappings, but I love the reason for the season more! I even love the work of getting prepared, doing whatever needs to be done to make it a fun, successful time with family and friends. When the day's work is done, I relax and think about my great nephew many years ago. He seemed intensely involved playing a board game with older members of his family. Suddenly, he'd had enough, and in his four-year-old wisdom declared, "Phew! I need an rest!"

If only we as adults were that tuned in. Enough is enough, then it is time for "an rest." I've got just the place for you! Jesus says in Matthew 11:28: "*Come to me, all you who are weary and burdened, and I will give you rest*" (NIV).

So in the midst of your busyness, whatever that looks like, take a few moments of quietness. Take a deep breath and remember that a little time of rest and relaxation will actually sprinkle a little more fun and excitement into your Christmas season! It will also give you the renewed energy you need to continue on your way to the party!

On the Way to the Party
CHRISTMAS: THE GOOD, THE SAD, AND THE SNUGLY!

I must say, Christmas has always been my favourite time of year. I'd like to share a couple of my memories with you. As a child, I always enjoyed Christmas … not because we had a lot in the material sense, but my family was large and always got together on that day.

One of my best memories of my young adult years came in the form of a young man! God brought him into my life at just the right time. He proposed on our second date (Boxing Day), and I said yes! Well, actually, it was more like "sure." Okay, we had known each other for nine years and had been good friends in our teens. We even dated a few times. Then after years of separation, the inevitable happened. By the following Christmas, we were married, and the first of our four babies was on his way.

Sadly, after thirty-four Christmases, cancer stole him from us. That last Christmas we brought him home from the hospital for forty-eight hours. All of our children and grandchildren were with us. It was good to be together, although there was a heavy, underlying sadness, knowing in our hearts that outside of a miracle (and I do believe in miracles, not only at Christmas), this would be the last time we would all be together. Three weeks later, my husband was promoted into the presence of the Lord and Saviour he loved and served.

Christmas changed for our family after that. Joy and meaning returned, but they took on a different hue. Four years later, I was a newlywed again. God had brought another wonderful man to me, and my family had more than doubled in size and capacity for fun! With all of our kids raising their own "young'uns," life becomes almost steroid-ridden when we get together—in a good way, of course. The smart retorts of the adults and older teens, the excitement of "middlers" pulling a fast one on an auntie or uncle (or most often Grandma), and let's not forget the adorable antics of the toddlers—put it all together and it's a yummy recipe for love and good times.

God loves family; He created the concept in the first place, and I believe nothing gives Him greater pleasure than to see His children following His example of loving and giving at any time of the year. There's no better opportunity to walk in love, acceptance, and forgiveness than as we meander side by side through this amazing phenomenon we call "family."

It all started on that very first Christmas. God sent His own son to this world to be born as a human so that we could, through Him, have a relationship with our creator, God. This was a good day for the human race; actually, all of heaven rejoiced! However, as a parent, I can't help but wonder if God Himself didn't feel a bit of sadness, knowing what His son would face: the nonchalance, the open rejection and abuse, culminating in a cruel death by crucifixion. He took this to buy us forgiveness, freedom, and victory.

But then I think that maybe God was seeing the end result of expanding His family. He desires to have a relationship with us, and that was made possible through Jesus' sacrifice on the cross.

Christmas may be a happy time for you, or it may invoke many sad memories. Maybe you feel the warmth of family and loving relationships, or maybe you feel very much alone. I invite you to join God's family; there's nothing like it. Let's take a hand and walk together on our way to the party!

On the Way to the Party
GOD INVENTED RECYCLING

Well, the main event of Christmas is over, and now we're just kind of floating in the haze of fatigue, sugar, and tryptophan until the bells ring in the New Year. Then, of course, life begins to pick up speed again! Actually, I'm also floating in a few tears after saying goodbye to my kids and grandkids again. They've all grown taller than me in the last year, and that's just wrong!

During the Christmas week, it seemed that every time I turned around, there was a pile of stuff to haul to the recycling bin. Now, I'm pretty old, and recycling is a pretty new concept as far as years go, yet I can't remember a time when it wasn't being done. When I was a child (just a few years ago), my mother didn't throw out a whole lot. She re-purposed, re-used, and re-beautified everything she could get her hands on! I love that she taught me to be frugal and creative. Okay, some people would call it cheap, but I like my terms for it! When "recycle" first became a buzz word, I thought, *Well, duh! It's been done.*

To be honest, my mom didn't come up with the idea either. It was all God's idea, part of His plan. If you're familiar with some of the more famous stories from the Bible, you'll remember that there was a time when God sent a little rain and made the entire world clean and new again. Or how about rebellious Jonah? He went for a swim (not his choice) and had a heart transformation in the belly of a big fish at the bottom of the sea. He had a whale of a time and came out of that experience a new man with a new purpose. Saul was a very bad man, and one day he saw the light; he changed direction, changed his name (to Paul), and changed his world! In 2 Corinthians 5:17, we're told that when we come to God through Jesus Christ, He makes us brand new. The old is *gone* and the new has come.

As we enter the new year ahead, let's think about it; let's adopt a new dream and a new purpose, one that will carry us through the year and keep us on track as we head on out on our way to the party.

On the Way to the Party
THE NEW VERSUS THE OLD

Less than a year ago, I was hospitalized for left knee replacement surgery. Having been told that it would be a painful recovery, and slower than usual because of issues in my right foot and ankle, I thought I was prepared. Well, words cannot describe! However, as healing progressed, and with the help of physiotherapy, function slowly returned to my left leg. It had been so stiff and painful for so long that after the initial pain of surgery, I began to see the light at the end of the tunnel. Hope drove me to continue pursuing my exercises at home. A few months after the procedure, we made a trip to Winnipeg, Manitoba to visit family.

My three grandsons, of course, were excited to see Grandma and Grandpa. The youngest, five-year-old Zeus, came up to me and hesitantly asked if he could see my knee. I proceeded to show him the incision line and, on his level, explain what the doctor had done. He was rather enthralled with the thought that there were new "parts" in there made of plastic and steel. He then asked if he could feel my knee, to which I replied "Of course!" Gently running his hand up and down and across, circling around, he looked up, puzzled, and stated, "Grandma, I can't feel any robot parts." Yes, I know, that's kind of cute and funny! I promise you, though, I know there are new parts in there. I can feel the difference, both in the absence of pain and the increased function.

Let's look at 2 Corinthians 5:17. Here, God's Word gives the promise that "… *if anyone is in Christ, he is a new creation; old things have passed away; behold, all things have become new.*" You wake up in the morning, look in the mirror, and gasp! The hair is still standing out in every direction, your ears are no smaller than before, and the zit on your chin looks like it had steroids for a snack the night before. We won't mention the number on the bathroom scale! Okay, I think we all know that the verse is referring to becoming a new person on the inside. In no way does this mean that we will automatically be different, but it does mean that the new parts, or potential, are there, thanks to a supernatural transplant that God alone can accomplish through His son, Jesus Christ. As we spend time in the presence of the master physiotherapist, and under His instruction and encouragement exercise the necessary changes, we get past that most painful phase and grow the difference in our thoughts, goals, and actions. Life becomes new and different!

How exciting to take a brief glance behind us and see where we've been, so that we can be truly thankful to God for where He has brought us. Adventure, change, and challenges lie ahead as we continue on our way to the party!

On the Way to the Party
THROW THAT STONE!

We were standing on the shore of the mighty Atlantic Ocean. Off in the distance, we could see several whales emitting their water spouts high in the air. Standing there and gazing across the water, I drew in a deep breath, savouring the moist, salt-scented air.

I had travelled to Newfoundland with my daughter and son-in-law. After the recent passing of my husband, it was good to feel needed again. It seemed that taking this trip with three little boys aged five, three, and three weeks definitely left me feeling needed. Tiny Fogo Island was a beautiful, relaxing place to spend a few weeks. Here I could focus on healing just a little more and spend quality time with family.

Suddenly, out of the silence came the voice of three-year-old Rambo. "Can I frow a stone in du river?"

Like for any of us, the attraction was in viewing the ever-widening circles left on the surface of the water as the stone sank to the bottom. I'm sure his three-year-old brain was imagining the amazing ripple effect while not quite registering the fact that a stone thrown "in du river" would make a lasting impact, forever changing the ocean.

Every stone thrown into the ocean by an innocent, unsuspecting little boy makes a difference! Let's think about that for a moment. Every unkind word or thoughtless deed that emanates from me makes a difference in someone's life. On the other hand, every positive act of kindness or encouraging word *also* changes the life of the person touched by it. This leaves me with a choice: do that one little thing to bring help and healing, extend that forgiveness, give that smile of encouragement in passing … or vent my feelings (knowing that only hurt can result from it) and withhold a caring attitude and heartfelt praise when someone needs the little pick me up?

In the sermon on the mount, Jesus challenges His followers to be salt and light in this world. It seems to follow, then, that if we claim to be His children, it should be evident in the way we carry ourselves and live out our lives. In a world so challenged by the bland, non-caring attitudes of many, and the darkness of evil directed too often at the most innocent, I say the choice to make is a no-brainer!

Let's choose to put some flavour and light into our lives and the lives of those around us; it will provide us joy and direction on the way to the party!

On the Way to the Party
THE POWER OF PRAISE

Because our family had just marked the anniversary of my first husband's death, this story is close to my heart and mind. During his illness and subsequent passing, we learned to lean heavily on the healing effect of praise music. The burdens of every day, no matter the size, seemed to shrink as I listened to the praises of our ever faithful and loving God. The problems and challenges grew smaller in comparison as my vision of a caring heavenly Father expanded. Music became my breath of life as I inhaled God's promises and exhaled His praise! It was my husband, Larry, who had set us firmly on this course.

Years earlier, our large two-story house was becoming rather empty as the kids were marrying and leaving home one at a time. The youngest of our four children was still living at home with us, and we thought it a good plan to have her move into the basement bedroom so we could return our second floor into the revenue apartment it was meant to be. With a private entrance already in place, there were minimal changes to be made.

We found good, dependable tenants, and all went smoothly for a while. Our third renter, however, was found deceased in the apartment after a hot Easter weekend. He had died of a gunshot wound. Some of us, reminiscing on the goings-on in the apartment during the wee hours of the morning, didn't believe it was self-inflicted, but the police at the scene quickly deemed it suicide. Regardless of how and why, our family was in a mind-numbing shock for weeks, and I might add somewhat paralyzed by fear. Our sense of personal safety had received a blow that was difficult to recover from.

My husband, being a strong man of God and a spiritual leader in our family, determined that the peace and joy in our home would *not* be stolen by Satan, the enemy of God and all that is good! He began playing praise and worship music constantly. As long as we heard the powerful words wafting through our home, the peace of Jesus Christ reigned. After a few weeks, it seemed that home was indeed home again, a shelter of warmth in a sometimes cold, cruel world, a soft place to land when things "out there" got hard.

So yes, he trained us well, and to this day I love listening to music, especially music that sets my heart in tune with my God and causes the Spirit of Christ to show up and walk with me through the challenges I face on my way to the party!

On the Way to the Party
FILLED BY FAITH

My first husband was self-employed for many years while our children were growing up. I ran a home daycare to help the family budget, so our income tended to fluctuate. Because of the nature of Larry's work, there were often slow-downs in the industry. One year when we were anticipating one such season, he reminded me of how God had led His people out of bondage and slavery in Egypt. They ended up in the desert, and for forty years God met their needs there. Understanding that God had a better life for us, we also knew that we needed provision as we walked through the dry places. We were learning to live in faith and victory over adverse circumstances, and part of that was learning to "speak to the mountain" in our life, whatever it happened to be. In Mark 11:23, Jesus states *"Truly I tell you, if anyone says to this mountain, 'Go, throw yourself into the sea,' and does not doubt in their heart but believes that what they say will happen, it will be done for them"* (NIV).

Knowing God's promise and believing it, we stood in faith as my husband pointed at the fridge and kitchen cabinets and boldly declared, "You are full of good, nutritious food. Every need is provided in Jesus Christ, and nothing is lacking!" Then he began to thank God for His provision. According to Philippians 4:19: *"And my God will meet all your needs according to the riches of his glory in Christ Jesus"* (NIV). Note the absence of complaining and self-pity. No reminding God of all our needs and problems, just thanking Him for doing what He promised in this passage.

I wish you could have popped in every Wednesday for the next four months! Within a week, we had a visit from a friend. She said that she was connected with an organization that was feeding the homeless. They needed someone to take some food off their hands every Wednesday (their intake day). Since they weren't able to use everything, a lot would go to waste. For some reason, she thought of us, and of course we said we could help, knowing that this was God's answer to our prayer.

For the next four months we drove down every Wednesday, late in the afternoon, and made a pick-up that filled our car (a three-seater station wagon)! God is good and He is faithful.

It doesn't end there. We knew some larger single-income families, some single-parent families, and some other families that could benefit from the help. A few phone calls, a bit of foot traffic, and we could finally see the kitchen floor again! Not only were we blessed, but because we took God at His Word, our needs were met weekly along with those of five other families!

But there's more! Another year, our freezer had just decided to quit, and again Larry pointed at the traitor and spoke in faith. The words were simply: "I declare we have a freezer that works and is full of meat." Within days, his nephew called from another town. He had a little problem; he needed a place to store a freezer for a while, and we could use it while it was being stored.

But there's more! The nephew happened to own a grocery store and was overloaded with meat that had been kept frozen since before the expiry date. He wondered if we could make use of it. Again, we saw God's answer to our need when we spoke in faith.

This isn't a directive or a formula, but when you know what God has promised, hang on to the promise in faith and walk in obedience to Him. Somehow, you'll always just happen to be in the right place at the right time. Unexpected bumps can rise up in the road, but God takes care of His own on the way to the party!

On the Way to the Party
SUMMER OF THE SQUIRREL

Today as I gaze longingly out of my kitchen window, my eyes see snow, snow, and more snow. Some is packed down tightly into icy ridges, some has drifted into white waves against the tree trunks, and a whole lot more is shoved into large, dirty, chunky piles along the walking path that runs along the back of our home. Yep, my eyes see snow; my mind, on the other hand, sees dry pavement cul-de-sac, dry concrete walk, and a lovely carpet of velvety green grass, generously dotted with trees of all types and sizes! Just beyond the fence I observe two little black balls of fluff romping cheerfully from tree to tree, up one, down another, and away out of sight. I sigh and return to my tasks, knowing they will be back after the break!

Shortly after settling into our new home early last summer, I noticed her for the first time. I glanced out of my kitchen window and there she was, creeping slowly and carefully along the top of the fence. When she reached the bird feeder hanging just above her head, she hesitantly stretched her head upwards but, alas, her face didn't fit into the tiny dispenser. I felt her desperation and deep disappointment as she tucked in her tail and dejectedly crawled down the chain link fence. I promptly made a quick trip to Walmart to purchase a bag of "proper" squirrel food. Again, I felt for her when she climbed the fence and found an inverted frisbee, full of treats just for her! This time her tiny black face and bright little eyes noticeably radiated joy and anticipation! She was large and chubby with scruffy, black fur. It wasn't until a few months later when a smaller, smoother version showed up that I realized there was a good reason for her chubby form.

As fall approached, I kept re-filling the feeder, and my guests kept coming, stuffing their cheeks, and hiding their treasures! Then one day I looked out and for the first time saw a large grey squirrel on the fence. He struck a pretty pose momentarily and then took off like lightning as a streak of black rushed in from nowhere!

Oh my! There's lots of food; you can share. Don't be such a bully!

I was instantly reminded of how some people react when we come close to realizing our dream. For some reason, they feel compelled to point out all the negatives, all the reasons why we shouldn't move ahead and claim our prize. And for what? Envy? Self-righteousness? Maybe a need to build themselves up by putting others down? Whatever the reason, don't let anyone chase you away from fulfilling the vision God has put on your heart!

Is there a black squirrel in your life? Maybe several? Guess what … they don't count. Keep your eyes on the prize and keep building the dream!

This is just a little something I learned on the way to the party!

On the Way to the Party
BLACK SQUIRREL, THE SQUEAKUEL

I loved watching my frisky little squirrel friends through the kitchen window. My daughter even dubbed the habit, "Mom's reality show." Seriously, it beats anything I ever saw on TV. I even imagined that we were starting to establish a bit of a relationship. Okay, don't go writing to Dr. Phil about that!

Fall was in full swing; the snow would soon be here to stay. One day my hubby went to the back of the house, and the squirrels didn't rush off as they usually did. They were becoming familiar and maybe just a little desperate to pack in more food for winter.

Well, this time our local maintenance man, Ross, was with him, and when my husband pointed out that I had been feeding the little critters all summer, Ross explained how destructive squirrels are and that they're prone to chew the coating off electrical wires. Thinking of the possible consequences, Larry then signed an "executive order" to have the feeder removed!

Needless to say, I was saddened by this, but at the same time, I understood. They don't come around anymore, they never call or write, and I can't find them on Facebook. They obviously don't really care about me! Never did! Now I'm beginning to realize that those cute little suckers are a lot like some people I've known—all because I don't feed them anymore.

How sad. I pray that I will never be that little rodent that simply takes advantage of others' kindness and then takes off and ignores them when the handouts stop coming. I want my relationships to go deeper than that, and I want to be friends to the end. I read in Proverbs 17:17: *"A friend loves at all times, and a brother is born for adversity."* I commit myself to being there for my friends, especially in the hard times, so we can arrive at the party together!

On the Way to The Party
JESUS INVENTED TWITTER

So tell me, who really invented Twitter? Before you go researching all the facts and figures, I do know what Google tells me. I beg to differ. Dorsey, Stone, Glass, and Williams may have brought it into the twenty-first century, but would you let me introduce you to someone who walked this earth over two thousand years ago? He made a few friends, and as He met them, He would say "Follow me." Many did and were not disappointed as they listened to what He had to say about life in general: relationships, business principles, and relating to their creator God in particular. Many listened, but not all actually followed Him.

Those that did follow found that He didn't promise a trouble-free life but rather that He would never leave them or forsake them (Hebrews 13:5). He also promised that "*I am with you always, even to the end of the age*" (Matthew 28:20b). That means we can count on Him through thick and thin, in good times and in bad, through anything life throws at us. Those words spoken thousands of years ago resound in our hearts today.

I've lived a few years, and as Dr. Phil says, "This ain't my first rodeo!" Yet I've found the promise of Jesus' constant presence and power in my life to be so much more than empty words. Yes, I follow Him, and I too have never been disappointed! Life is good, albeit never stress free.

Heartache and disappointment, crushed dreams and daily challenges have been my travelling companions all my life. But the presence of Jesus Christ is with me, and I invite you to join me as I continue to follow Him on the way to the party!

On the Way to the Party
WHEN A FRIEND DIES

Some time ago, my world was shaken when a good friend called to inform me of the death of their youngest son, a young man in his mid-twenties and full of life and energy. But he was more than just a friend ... he was my godson. I'd known him and loved him from the day he was born. I'd sewn an infant-size outfit for him, and if you know me, you know what a labour of love that was. A seamstress I'm not! I was so in love with the little guy, I just didn't see that a store-bought gift involved the same investment of love.

I knew the parents were crushed and devastated, literally heart-broken. For days a heaviness I could not escape rested on me. To make matters worse, I opted not to attend the memorial service. I would have had to fly to another province, and upon my return, go directly to the hospital for surgery. I knew I would need all my strength, physical and emotional, for optimum recovery. I waffled for days on that decision and finally did the wise thing and stayed home—and wept! I don't think I ever touched the heart of Jesus like I did that week, remembering that He in His human form hurt so badly when His friend died that He wept too.

Now I don't know about you, but I've said some pretty dumb things in an effort to be comforting, and I've heard some dumb things. One thing that has become clear to me is that it's *always* okay and acceptable just to *be* there, eyes open and alert, to *see* little things that need to be done, and then *do* them. Above all, if you dare to say, "Let me know if you need anything" (and I wouldn't recommend that approach), please be prepared to fulfill the request. It's only an empty platitude otherwise!

It's good to grieve and weep for a season. But like Jesus at the graveside of His friend Lazarus, after weeping we must take that one step further and bring life back into the situation. Not all of us will raise the dead back to life, but all of us, by the grace of God, are able to bring life-filled words to someone's aching heart. In sowing the seeds of life and joy, we can literally see the hurting come back to life when they feel as if they too had died.

On life's pathway we may often stumble and fall, stub our toes and scrape our knees. Let's get up again, embrace life, and continue on the way to the party!

On the Way to the Party
FORTY YEARS … AND I CAN ONLY IMAGINE!

My mom! Many years ago, she was promoted into the presence of Jesus. I still miss her! Sometimes I stop and think about her and how she delighted in her grandchildren. She anticipated the coming of new babies with utmost joy. After they arrived, she'd often spend days or weeks helping out so the young family could get back on their feet, literally. She looked forward to the married kids' visits, knowing they would bring the little ones, and in preparation for that time kept herself busy baking special treats or sewing up some little thing that would delight the heart of any little girl and her doll!

One little guy especially loved Grandma's porridge cookies, and there was always a generous supply of those. I honestly have no idea how she did it all with so many of us still at home; I'm the youngest of thirteen! I suppose that's why she never seemed to take that much delight in her own children. She was too busy taking care of us. Even then I never doubted her love for all of us. I remember her as a very hard worker, putting in long hours every day, often to her own detriment. There wasn't much time or energy for her to exhibit a bubbling enjoyment in motherhood.

I remember times when patience was thin and I heard sharp words flying like swords from her mouth. This usually happened in the face of snarky, teenage comments coming from me or my brothers. Through it all I always knew I was loved by her.

She was wheelchair-ridden by the time I got married as a young adult. I felt a deep loss for all the things we couldn't do and enjoy together in that season of my life. When my first baby was born, I missed her physical presence incredibly. When we visited with the new baby, she never failed to show a special interest in him and all his care. I am so thankful to God that she was still there to offer some much-appreciated advice and encouragement! As long as she lived, she was there when I needed her wisdom and guidance. As a child it was enough at times just to quietly crawl alongside each other in the dirt as we weeded the garden together.

Today when I think of her, I can still see her sitting in the living room in her favourite chair. In her aproned lap lies an open Bible, and her head is bowed in prayer. Seeing her like that made me feel safe, knowing that she was praying for her children and grandchildren. How do I know? I can still feel the strength of those prayers, and I see the effects in the lives of my children and grandchildren. It inspires and challenges me to add my prayers to hers and make an even greater difference in the lives of my offspring.

In being a godly mom, she threw a stone in the river, and the ripples of her influence are still being seen and felt today. My mom wasn't perfect, but she was perfect for me!

So it's not Mother's Day, but we all can and should give tribute to our moms any and every day of the year. It seems a good time to do that as I remember the day she arrived at the party forty years ago!

As for me, I'm still on the way to the party.

On the Way to the Party
TOO BLESSED TO BE STRESSED

In March of 2011, about six weeks after the passing of my husband of thirty-five years, I was living in the thick fog of grief. Some very good friends from Texas sent me an invitation to join them for a while. It was a sweet opportunity to step out of the usual aftermath of death in the family. The purpose wasn't to run away—that's just not me! I would rather embrace the storm and all the pain it brings and plow through, at the same time recognizing that everyone deals with grief in their own way. I knew this trip and the short time away would give me a fresh perspective on what I was going through and the "new normal" I was about to embark on.

One day while I was there, my friend Wanda took me to an antique mall. Part of the mall was simply set up as a unique boutique with new items for sale. My eyes were drawn to a lovely black bag; down each side ran a white with black polka dot ribbon topped with a bow. It featured embroidery on one side that spoke to me: "Too blessed to be stressed." I couldn't decide right there, but I asked her to take me back a few days later. That beautiful bag now lives in my closet, and I still use it! The beauty isn't necessarily in the item itself but rather in the constant reminder that, indeed, I am too blessed to be stressed!

In Jeremiah 29:11, God makes a promise to all who believe and follow Him. His thoughts toward us are always and only good. The promise includes peace, hope, and a future! With that in mind, I can't help but understand how truly blessed I am. In the midst of stressful circumstances, I don't need to live in the stress. As I lean into God's promises, focusing on the blessings in my life, I continue on my way to the party!

On the Way to the Party
A NEW BABY MEANS WORK!

There's nothing like holding a squishy, squirmy little bundle for the first time! When I think back to the births of my own babies, all four of them, I have to admit that I *really* loved the helpless newborn stage. Many people say that they'd just as soon wait until they're presented with a curious little three-year-old. Yes, those demanding little creatures can be quite intimidating; I loved it! Have you ever noticed how much work is involved? If done properly, raising children, nurturing and teaching them, is an intense undertaking!

Hopefully by the time they can be trusted to walk to the next block to play with friends you can be confident they'll get there and return home safely at the specified time.

During these very young years, we often make the mistake of trying to be "super mom" and do it all ourselves. While that seems to be a noble endeavour, we need to relinquish a little control and allow others to lend a hand in order to gain the most rewarding outcome. This doesn't diminish our importance in baby's life; rather, it adds a dimension to the small child's life that can broaden and help to develop facets of their personality. Also, think of the blessing and fulfilment received by those who contribute to your little one's life.

When I think of the joy I've experienced taking care of babies (in twenty-two years of home daycare), it brings to mind how God, my heavenly Father, must feel when "babies" join His family! In the same way, when we guide others into the family of God, they can't be left on their own. They need our love and acceptance right where they are, along with a good dose of forgiveness when they stumble and fall. They need our constant prayer, support, and verbal encouragement.

At times we may need to take it a step further and bring in an outside source of help, or specialized therapy. A counsellor trained to deal with trauma and ugly baggage from the past can be an asset. They can help to propel the new "child" to a life of fulfilment and destiny achieved for the glory of God!

I just want to encourage you to keep having those babies and bring them with you on the way to the party!

On the Way to the Party
SPRING IN MY STEP

It's that time of year again! You look around the house and catch sight of bits of clutter here and there, stuff that wasn't there a few months ago. Yes, it happens every week. A few flyers get tossed into the magazine rack and, in no time, they start reproducing. And you thought rabbits had the corner on that! Your closets now hold things you've grown out of one direction or the other. Those tired, whimsical little must-haves have now become must-gos!

When spring comes to my town, I happily stuff the heavy winter cushions and candles, hangings and home decor items, into bins and closets. Then I bring out the lights and brights of spring and summer. I actually look forward to that special moment and literally *make* myself wait for just the right day. When it's all done, I enjoy the new look, and it makes me feel lighter and brighter!

I wonder if God looks at me sometimes and sees the clutter and drab heaviness I've allowed to cling to me. As I think of it, I'm quite aware of a tiny bit of envy, a tinge of impatience, or a wee dribble of resentment. Not much of anything, really, but altogether it creates a look that is less than appealing and leaves less room for love, acceptance, and forgiveness for others. So I stuff all these undesirables in a "has bin" and give them to God. He then buries them in a sea of forgetfulness and gives me a new life, complete with fresh attitudes and a lighter, brighter outlook. And yes, this exchange has to happen frequently. Then with a spring in my step, I can continue on my way to the party!

On the Way to the Party
GOD DOESN'T CARE!

Some time ago, my husband and I attended a gospel music concert. One of the groups, Greater Vision, introduced one of their songs with the title, "God Doesn't Care." Hold on a minute! That's not what I've been taught all my life. Yes, there have been those times when for a short while I even thought that myself. However, my Bible tells me in Jeremiah 29:11 that God knows the plans He has for me, plans to prosper me and not to harm me, plans to give me a hope and a future. Many other verses carry a similar message. So when someone says, "God doesn't care," I have to disagree wholeheartedly.

Wait a minute! The song goes on to speak about all the stuff in my life that fails to honour the God who created me: the basic sin of rebellion, nasty attitudes toward those in authority, gossiping about one friend to another, and we can't forget the sins of lust, debauchery, and disrespect to family members.

Okay! I get it. He doesn't care about my past sin or about what I've done; He just wants to love me! When all my sin and failures are put under the cleansing blood of Jesus, they're gone. When they are confessed and repented of, I am forgiven and clean again, according to 1 John 1:9.

That's why we celebrate Good Friday. As sad and dark a day as it was, through Jesus' sacrificial death on a cruel cross, I can face God and feel only the warmth of His love radiating out toward me! He doesn't care who, where, or what I was. By the same power that raised Christ from the dead, He has made me a brand-new person, a new creation.

So you see, what has transpired in the past no longer defines who I am, nor does it bind me with chains that deny me the freedom of God's plan for my life. God doesn't care, and I couldn't agree more!

The question remains: What will you do about it? I choose to love and follow Him with all my heart. Even having made that commitment, I fail Him often, but how awesome it is to remember that God doesn't care about the sin and failures that are brought before Him and forgiven. He does care about *me*, and He does care about *you*!

Being confident of His loving care is what keeps me going as I continue on the way to the party!

On the Way to the Party
THE LONG WINDING ROAD TRIP

After months of planning and preparing for this, I am finally here! Of course, my first priority in planning a trip that crosses two provinces is to visit my kids and grandchildren. The second reason is to present my books, which have both been published within the past two years. This trip, though, I have arranged to meet up with old friends as well, to touch base and catch up. A few days ago, for instance, I had dinner with a friend I met almost sixty years ago. Whew! I had no idea that would make me sound *so* old!

After arriving at my daughter's house and indulging myself in grandson hugs for several days, I dropped off my husband at the airport to catch his flight home and then took off across the country to play "catch-up." My first road trip adventure involved a call to CAA to please kindly unlock my car so I could get at my keys and hopefully gain access to my luggage!

No trip is ever complete without getting lost, despite very clear directions. Because it was a rural address, I didn't use the GPS; actually, I didn't use her because I really don't like her. She's competition. It seems she's always vying for my hubby's attention when we're out driving. Poor guy ... with two women constantly telling him where to go, it's amazing he's still got all his wits about him!

My next stop was a delightful little town where an old friend from high school resides. She and her husband host a weekly Bible study in their home—with quite a turnout, I might add. Here I had the opportunity to speak some words of encouragement and hope to people, all of whom are going through the "stuff" of life.

After I was done speaking, my friend, Lois, served refreshments, and we all had a chance to chat. As I was in the midst of an intense conversation, my cup of coffee suddenly developed a mind of its own and ended up … you guessed it … all over me! After the first few stunned seconds, laughter erupted and all were in agreement that they would not soon forget the guest speaker who got so excited she "wet herself!"

Today a three-hour drive brought me back to loving little-boy hugs! Oh yes … and one big boy hug from the one who's not so little any more! Ahhh! There's nothing like it.

Yes, life is an exciting journey, but it's not the end of the road. We have yet to arrive; we're still on the way to the party!

On the Way to the Party
ON THE ROAD AGAIN (STILL)

So there we were, driving east about forty-five minutes away from home. I was very excited about seeing my daughters, son-in-law, and grandsons in Winnipeg. Then the thought hit me: I was also looking forward to doing some book signings and promotional meetings in Manitoba. Oh *no*! I turned to my husband and in total shock said, "Honey, we have to turn around and go back home."

I don't think he believed me, and he probably thought I was pulling an April Fool's joke on him. (I've been known to do that!) He found a place to turn around on the busy highway, and nearly two hours later we were back at the same spot, heading east, but this time with extra boxes of books in the back of the car! I always carry a few in a tote bag, but that would not have been enough for what I was attempting to do.

You always hear the talk about getting older and starting to forget some things from time to time. I'm not convinced it's age as much as brain overload and failure to properly manage it. Whatever it is, I thank God for a sweet husband who just calmly turned the car around and headed back to do what had to be done!

All that time I was thinking, *Well, God has a bad memory too, so I'm in good company!* When I confess my sins to God, my Bible tells me that He casts them into the sea (Micah 7:19), or He removes them from me as far as the east is from the west (Psalm 103:12). That's kind of far! It goes so far as to say in Hebrews 8:12b: "… *their sins and their lawless deeds I will remember no more*" (emphasis added). Okay, so this probably refers to the fact that after we confess our sins and repent, or change direction, God no longer holds our sins against us. Through Jesus' death on the cross, they were paid for, and we have the opportunity to be redeemed, or bought back by God, if we so choose. In any case, I have made that choice and now am definitely in good company!

The rest of the trip has been fun, enjoyable, and enlightening as I have been meeting up with old friends and watching my grandsons grow up and achieve new heights on a daily basis. Oh, and of course having a few hugs and cuddles thrown in here and there doesn't hurt. I've certainly enjoyed doing the book promotion. Besides being able to sell my books, there's always the expectation that someone will be encouraged and more hopeful after hearing me speak or reading one of my books.

A few days ago as I was driving west on Regent Avenue, on what I hoped would be a quick little shopping trip, I ran into a snag. I was stopped at a train crossing, and the lights continued to blink their warnings and the safety arms remained down long after the train had passed through. As I waited and waited and the line behind me got longer and longer, it became apparent that there was a major malfunction. I was trapped in traffic. Being on the inside lane, I seriously considered driving over the curb, across the median, and down the other curb. I decided it wasn't worth the risk to my vehicle, so I just waited. After about fifteen minutes (which felt like hours), some young men from cars behind me jumped out of their vehicles and ran up to the crossing. Shortly after, the line of cars started to move, and I realized what had happened.

As I crossed the tracks, I saw them standing on either side of the lanes and physically holding up the arms! I thought of the story in the Bible where Moses found it necessary to hold out his arms toward his people as they fought a battle against the enemy. As long as he held out his arms, they prevailed. However, when his arms got tired, they fell behind. Other men came alongside him and held up his arms for him. Needless to say, the enemy was trounced!

Maybe someone today could use your strength to hold up their arms. I've been challenged in my own life lately to keep my eyes and heart wide open, because they are out there, just waiting and needing a little boost from me. Maybe from you too!

In three days I will be home, rejoining my dear husband as together we continue on the way to the party!

On the Way to the Party
NOTICE THE SIGNS

It was a long, lonely road. Somehow, I didn't really feel the loneliness in my very depths. I love music, so the hours on the road were basically one very long sing-along, and a loud one at that! I was extremely grateful for clear, sunny days and a dry highway. Put that all together with the fact that I was on my way home, and my joy could not be dampened.

I had just left my two daughters, son-in-law, and three young grandsons in Winnipeg after spending two weeks there. As I drove away from their house and turned the corner at the end of their street, the tears flowed freely. I missed them already and knew that "my" boys would have grown up so much more by the time I saw them again. By the time I reached the city's perimeter highway, the tears were gone and I was settling in for the many miles ahead, a smile lighting my face, because my real life awaited me at the end of the road.

As I travelled, I looked forward to seeing the mileage signs: to Brandon, Regina, Swift Current, Medicine Hat, Brooks, and finally Calgary! The downward trend in the numbers became a continual lift to my spirits as I sailed west!

Shortly after I passed Regina, the flat tablelands began to disappear, and the gently rolling hills began. That's when I really sat up and took notice. It was definitely one of the signs that I was nearing home! The gentle rolls became a little more distinct and decisive as I continued west of Swift Current, aka Speedy Creek!

About this time, I began to be on the lookout for wildlife alongside the road, because it was the place where "the deer and the antelope play" (mostly the antelope). That is, if you can spot them. They are cleverly clothed in coats that blend so beautifully with the dry, brown grass of the hills this time of year.

And there it was—that scenic dip into the South Saskatchewan River valley at the west end of Medicine Hat! I always look forward to that part of the drive. Not only is it a beautiful spot, but it brings me to less than three hours from home!

As I rolled steadily toward the end of the trip and my arrival home, I couldn't help but think about this road we're all on called LIFE. Are we enjoying the ride? Are we just dragging our way through because it's something we have to do? Or do we make the most of every opportunity? Do we give it our all as we look forward to our final, forever home?

The signs of my imminent arrival at home kept popping up more and more frequently. In no time, it seemed, I'd arrived and found myself in the arms of the one I love!

One of these days the road of life will end for me, and I'll find myself in the loving arms of my heavenly Father, who right now is standing and cheering me on, urging me to look around and watch for the signs that Home is near.

In Mathew 24, Jesus' disciples ask Him to tell them the sign of His return and the end of the age. Jesus proceeds to teach them. If you read through the chapter, you'll find a lot of signs listed that we "see" or hear about every day on the news, and they are increasing in frequency and intensity, just like labour pains, which is what Jesus likens them to.

As we travel this road, let's be aware of the signs around us that point us toward home. Before we know it, we will arrive. Right now, we're on the way *to* the party!

On the Way to the Party
MANUAL OR MANNA?

Manual or manna? A one-time read or an everyday feed?
There are those who read the Bible, God's Word to us, in order to gain knowledge of historical events, or maybe to build an argument on any given topic. Some may read it as a ritual, following along in a religious service, or they may treat is as a horoscope reading, hoping for a little guidance for the day. Face it, making decisions is often difficult. If there's an easy way out, take it.

I don't think any of those reasons are wrong. I like to compare it to purchasing a piece of furniture from Ikea. Yeah, it comes in a box, so my temptation is to shove it into the corner in my bedroom, drape a runner over the top, and use it as a dresser. After all, that's what the box says it is. But in order to get maximum usage out of it, I need to take all the pieces out of the box, read the instructions, and use the recommended tools. In the end, I'll have a chest that actually has usable drawers for storing various items of clothing!

When God led the children of Israel through the desert thousands of years ago, He also provided them with manna on a daily basis. There was no other food available except for the quail, which was also supernaturally provided by God. This was their sustenance; without it, they would have died of starvation. Yes, our puny minds can't understand, but I believe it simply because I have put my faith in this God and choose to believe.

I go to the Word of God every day and read it, meditate on it as a cow chews her cud, ingest it into my spirit, and let it become my spiritual sustenance. It gives me strength and brings joy, peace, and comfort. And yes, it gives direction too! It teaches about long-ago happenings and situations and provides answers to questions. Here's the good news—it's not limited to any one of those things. When taken in every day, God's Word becomes my miracle manna, slowly but steadily changing me on the inside until my outside bears the evidence.

I have seen people literally come out of a shell of fear, low self esteem, and lack of self confidence by daily taking in the manna of God's Word and letting it do its work in them. This is the work of a miracle. All too often if our finite human minds can't figure it out, we think we have the option of choosing what we'll believe and what we'll leave behind. So how do I decide which part of the Bible is true and which part isn't? I feed on it daily and love its truth more every day. It is my strength, my joy, my peace, my companion, and my direction.

I have made the choice to believe. Period. I will continue to believe it all the way to the party.

On the Way to the Party
STONE SOUP ... FOR THE SOUL

Years ago, when my children were little, we had the children's classic *Stone Soup* in our home. The last time I remember seeing it, the pages were falling out and the hard cover looked rather beat up! Needless to say, it had been read a few times.

The story is about two cute, chubby little pigs travelling down the road. They begin to get hungry, so when they arrive at a village, they try to find food. But, alas, no one will share. They hatch the most brilliant idea! They get a huge pot, fill it with water, and throw in some stones. Then they begin to stir the pot. Whenever anyone comes by, they make a big deal of how delicious the soup will be. As villagers come to check it out, the little pigs comment on how it would be so much better if they could only have some onions, carrots, or meat. Bit by bit the people return with all the ingredients needed to create a delicious pot of soup. In the end, everyone is well fed, including the hungry little pigs!

Lately I've been thinking of that book. Why? I've been working with my cousin to plan a family reunion for this coming summer. Just when we had contacted all the people we could think of, we thought of more, so out went another email. After that, we thought of more, and so on. Now I think we may have exhausted the potential!

We're all from the same family, yet no two of us look the same, dress the same, or act the same. We come in a boundless variety of flavours, and we each add something of value to the pot. The soup would be somewhat bland without an onion or salt, and the family would not be the same without Billy or Joe.

So as I look forward to meeting all my cousins that I haven't seen for a long time, and those I may have met at one time but can't remember, I also anticipate a few differences of opinion, a few lively discussions, and some zesty comments! Yes, we all come from the same garden, but different rows. We all have roots but show a little differently. In the end, love, acceptance and forgiveness reign when we can't seem to agree with everything and everyone.

I don't know about you, but I plan to enjoy the soup created by my family—immediate, extended, in-laws, and steps. I will enjoy the delicious aroma and the nutrition it brings to my soul as I travel on, heading toward the party!

On the Way to the Party
CALLING ALL MOTHERS!

Need I remind you? Yes, it's Mother's Day again. I think it's a wonderful opportunity to focus on mothers and all they've brought to our lives. I dare say most of us spend many days of the year remembering those who brought us into the world and set our feet on the path we currently walk. I realize we grow up, make our own decisions, and set our plans and goals. However, the direction those plans take us in has an awful lot to do with the direction our parents, and mothers in particular, have set us on. Today I wish to pay tribute to the generations that have gone before, as well as those who will carry the torch forward, and all of us in between.

My mother bore and raised a large family, of which I am the youngest. She did it all with very little in the way of convenience or financial resources. I believe I mentioned earlier how she was, in my eyes, one of the world's first and greatest recyclers. One thing that stands out to me is her ability to look at a picture of a dress in a catalogue and make her own pattern, sew the dress, and make a matching hat (just like the Queen)! She was always well dressed. She taught me all I know about homemaking, baking, and cooking. Our home wasn't always spotless, but one of her favourite sayings was "a home should be clean enough to be healthy, and messy enough to be happy." I've tried to live by that rule, but I fear that many times I may have gotten a little too concerned about the clean part!

I was blessed with a wonderful mother-in-law who raised a great young man! I could never understand all the mother-in-law jokes floating around, since I had such a sweet lady in my life, always accepting and generous in every way. Her life is best expressed in the phrase she loved to quote: "Praise the Lord anyway." More than words, she lived her life in that attitude! Now I have another mother-in-law whom I never met. She also had a hand in raising a wonderful man, and through the stories I've been told, I've come to wish that I could have met her in this life.

With all these stellar examples who have walked the motherhood path before me, I've gained a few insights into this blessed world of "Mom." I hope I've learned a little bit about how to love my children in ways that assure them they are loved. If I love and they don't feel loved, I have loved in vain. I've learned that love doesn't always say yes. Sometimes the healthiest way is to say no and show acceptance and comfort until acceptance has taken root in them. I've learned that it's okay to lighten up and laugh with my kids and now my grandkids. I'm convinced that nothing brings them more joy than to see how they can put a smile on Mom or Grandma's face!

Even as a young girl, all I wanted to be when I grew up was a wife and mother. Looking back now, I can hardly believe how blessed I've been to be and do that. I feel empowered to look back and see how those before me built a foundation on which I could raise my own family. I learned so much from them and tried to teach it forward. I now see my children following many of the same patterns, as well as establishing some of their own. This is good and healthy.

Today I have eight amazing daughters and daughters-in-law. I love to see how they relate to their offspring, each one different from the other in detail but drawing from the same well of ethics and values. How refreshing to see how they take a moment to calmly teach their little ones (and those not so little) the realities of life, at the same time offering understanding and direction. I take note as to how age-appropriate boundaries are applied, and then as the children grow, the parameters are spread further afield, granting more freedom.

It takes a little insight to see that as children begin to grow up, their self esteem is bolstered when they can prove responsibility. I stand with pride as I observe, not because I did anything. No, the pride is solely placed in the younger generation for the decisions and choices they are making in the face of a society that challenges their values at every turn.

Because these awesome women are taking their responsibility seriously and raising young ones who will in turn become the next generation of parents, I can look forward with great anticipation to the day when I will see them parenting their own. Right now, my hands are off for the most part, and hopefully my mouth is shut! I promise you, though, that my heart is open, and as needs arise, they are lifted in prayer to the One who can make the *real* difference!

My hat goes off to every mother out there, whether you're just starting out or you're already battle-weary and trying to guide your kids through the turbulent teens. To you I say make great memories so that you have something to anchor to on those not-so-good days. If you have a relationship with Jesus Christ, stay close to Him and spend time in His Word, seeking His wisdom and committing your loved ones to His care.

God's Word says children are a gift from Him! May God bless you as you take care of that gift! We from the generation before stand behind you and walk beside you on the way to the party!

On the Way to the Party
SERVICE WITH A SMILE

It was a bright, crisp Saturday morning as we stood at our back door chatting out a long goodbye with our departing guests. Every few minutes I glanced into the kitchen, trying to keep an eye on our youngest child, then two. With an inward chuckle I followed her progress as she began to clear the breakfast table. One dish at a time she cleared away the morning's muck and mire. (We have four kids, okay?) I couldn't help but notice that the smile on her face was getting bigger and bigger! I couldn't believe it! I'm sure our ten-year-old would have balked at cleaning up after breakfast for eight, but this was her day to shine, and she took full advantage as step by step she whittled that mountain down to less than a mole hill.

When the table was done, she knew the next step was to push it back into its place in the corner and place the chairs around it. Even here, she pushed and strained at the enormous task until my "superior" strength took over and lightened her burden. Job completed, she happily toddled off to play with her toys, with that same beautiful smile still on her face! I will never forget that sweet example of joyful service.

I have to ask myself: When was the last time I was willing to serve my family, community, or church with such cheerful abandon? Or did I serve under duress, all the while thinking begrudgingly of the cost in time, cash, or energy? Thinking of that tiny moment in my life brings me to this conclusion: I want to be like a child when I'm faced with a task that may be just a bit too big for me. My Father in Heaven has promised His help and strength for every occasion. When it seems that I'm called on to do the dirty work, I want to do the job with a smile on my face, taking it one step at a time if necessary.

Have you heard the riddle: How do you eat an elephant? The answer is "One bite at a time." That's the only way to handle some situations in our lives. But remember, there's always One who is bigger, stronger, and more capable. You can count on Him to come alongside you and get 'er done! In Colossians 3:23–24, Paul says:

> *Whatever you do, work at it with all your heart, as working for the Lord, not for human masters, since you know that you will receive an inheritance from the Lord as a reward. It is the Lord Christ you are serving.* (NIV)

And serving is what I plan to do as I continue on the way to the party!

On the Way to the Party
BLOOM WHERE YOU'RE PLANTED

Okay, so I'll just tell you straight up—I love flowers, all kinds of flowers! Short ones, tall ones, and those in the middle, none escape my attention. Flowers with a gentle, pretty scent, those with a stronger, somewhat pungent aroma, and some that are even downright unpleasant. Yet every one of them contributes to the beauty of our world!

That said, I don't consider myself a green thumb in any way. All I'm capable of doing is digging a hole of the appropriate size and plunking the tiny plant into it. (Sometimes I even manage to get it to remain in a roots-down position!) Then I simply wait for sunshine and rain, in proper proportions, to do their part in raising it up to become a mature plant, proving itself in the revealing of its fruit. In this case, lovely blooms—some small, others larger—will show up and make me proud!

One thing I have to keep in mind is that some plants love shade and if placed in full sunlight will shrivel up and die, or at least not flourish. Those plants that are designed to grow in full sun won't develop properly in the shade and most certainly won't bloom to maximum potential. Having thought this through and planned accordingly, I then need to decide what to plant where. I certainly must not take a low growing border, such as alyssum or portulaca, and put it next to the house, with a poppy or Shasta daisy in front of it. However, take the poppy and plant it behind the shorter growth, and you have the beginnings of a beautiful little flower garden!

I haven't even started on the lovely scented evening breeze that assails my nostrils as I sit on my deck enjoying the sunset. I close my eyes as I lay my head back and begin to meditate, my thoughts turning automatically to the place where it all started. God had a plan way back then, a plan for me and the direction my life should take, even as I plan what my flower garden will look like. Just as I see it in my mind, so He saw me, according to Psalm 139!

He has a purpose for me; He has a purpose for you. Jeremiah 29:11 states: *"For I know the plans I have for you ... plans to prosper you and not to harm you, plans to give you a hope and a future"* (NIV). As that thought wends its way through my brain, I realize anew that I have no wish to be in the sun if my proper place of fulfillment is in the shade. If my place to bloom is supposed to be along the front border, I'm happy to be short (literally)! We can't all be poppies. Maybe there are enough out there with "tall poppy" syndrome who just haven't found their place to bloom yet.

I guess we all need to be in the "Son" to reach our full bloomin' potential! And that's right where I intend to stay as I make my way to the party!

On the Way to the Party
TIME TO DEADHEAD

So today we're still on the winding path through the flower garden. As much as I love the large colourful blooms and the sweet aroma floating subtly on the breeze, I dislike the chore of pulling off the spent blossoms. It's time consuming and it smacks of dealing with something lifeless, useless, and smelly. Better times have been had!

Every time I read advice on gardening, or watch a video that I hope will broaden my knowledge and produce a prettier sight, I cannot escape it. They all stress the importance of discarding the dead flowers in order to make room for new growth. This reminds me of a scripture verse, Colossians 3:5–10. Ephesians 4:22–24, 31 and 1 Peter 2:1 also speak of getting rid of old habits and behaviours. Why is this so important for a child of God? I don't consider myself a theologian, but my heart immediately tells me that things like anger, envy, resentment, hatred, lying, or gossip have no place in my life if I desire to see love, forgiveness, joy, and compassion bloom.

It's no secret that people are drawn to the sweetness of Jesus and the power of a living God in my life rather than the stinky old works of the enemy of God and His children! My mind goes quickly to all the useless, life-sucking tendencies exhibited in my life. Indeed, it is time to cut these off (the Bible talks about "putting off") and allow the life to flow into more positive, productive pursuits.

When I actually make the effort to get out there and pull off the withered blooms, it's amazing how fast those areas fill up with new flowers, and the pots and shrubs continue to look beautifully appealing throughout the entire summer!

Can you see yourself there? Take a moment to reflect and meditate. Read the scriptures listed above and see what that might look like in your life. I know that I want people I meet to look at me and be drawn not to me but to the God who made me to bear His beauty and character in this life. I want to bring goodness and light to a world that is hurting, but in order to do that, I must let go of all the dead weights that hinder me and allow the new growth to take place.

This will keep me busy along the path as I continue on to the party!

On the Way to the Party
ON A PEDESTAL

Oops! I blew it! I fell off …

Has this ever happened to you? A year ago, after moving to our current location, I found the space lacking for my short, white Grecian pillar that I used to use in my living room as a plant stand. I decided it would look just as beautiful outside with a trailing, flowering plant on it. I was right. It was gorgeous, giving a refreshing, brightly-coloured break to the backdrop of grey railings.

Shortly after I set it up, the winds came, something I had not anticipated. I'm not sure why, since our location is known for its sudden weather changes as well as the winds that howl their way through the city. I awoke in the morning and stepped out to survey my colourful kingdom. To my utter dismay, the lovely potted plant had toppled to the ground! Lifting it and placing it back on its pedestal, I noticed that many of the tiny stems were broken and ragged looking, and several of the pretty blooms were broken off. Not only that, but a couple of handfuls of potting soil had been lost in the grass. I was saddened to see the destruction of what had been such a tale of beauty the day before.

Have you ever found yourself on a pedestal not of your own making? It's a scary place to be, isn't it? I'm sure we've all been there at one time or another. I think I was probably up there in all of my children's minds, at least until the age of three or so!

I do know there was a time a wind came along and I toppled; it hurt, and it was humiliating. I would much rather be on the same level as others and feel stable and secure. In all fairness, I certainly don't try to put myself on a pedestal, and anyone else who is deluded enough to place me there deserves to feel like a schmuk when I do the proverbial face plant!

I try hard not to deify people; we are all human and prone to fall and fail. The first two of the Ten Commandments warn us not to have any god but the one true God, and I believe that if we commit to that alone, we will save ourselves a lot of heartache.

I'm not sure about you, but I'm keeping both my feet on solid ground as I head toward the party!

On the Way to the Party
LOOK WHO'S DRIVING!

Wasn't it just last week I took him out for lunch? And I watched with amusement as he meticulously broke his french fries in little pieces and dropped them over the side of his high chair. Even back then his sense of adventure and fun was greater than his appetite! After "eating" our lunch, I took him back to our house, where I set him on the floor and gave him freedom to just roam for a while. As an inquisitive one year old, he was happy to oblige.

Minutes later, I heard a quiet, fretful whimpering. I followed the sound and … couldn't find a thing! I kept silent for a moment and realized that the soft, panicked sounds were emanating from behind the couch. Set mere inches from the wall, it left a gap just wide enough for an average-size one year old to crawl in. (We realized later he was chasing a ball that went astray.) Once in, he was trapped! He hadn't yet mastered the art of backing up, and there was no room to turn around!

My grandma heart was a little saddened to imagine his fear of being trapped there, yet I had to chuckle as Grandpa and I proceeded to move the couch and free our little scamp!

As a grandparent, I have always tried to imagine how my grandchildren will fare as they grow up in this world, which is sometimes a scary thought. If I didn't know that I can trust them to a higher authority, I don't know how I'd survive their growing years. I know the One whose eye is on them at all times and who will keep them in His care, even when parents and grandparents can't. My heart is ready to explode with love and pride as I watch them take one step after another toward mature adulthood!

Take this morning, for instance. I just arrived yesterday for a short visit and hadn't seen these kids for six months, and the changes were amazing! We went on an errand earlier today, and I watched in awe as my oldest grandson got behind the wheel for the drive home. Way to go, Zac! He did a super job, right down to backing out of the parking spot (he's got that down pat), shoulder checking, signalling … the whole works. My first thought was, *When did this happen?* They move away, I blink, and here we are!

I think that maybe God looks at His kids with the same kind of love and pride, emitting the same expressions of encouragement while causing us to grow and expand our abilities with confidence. And one day we are given the wheel. Probably we won't do it all perfectly, but with practice we get better at doing the adult thing and making mature decisions.

As we go through life, let's remember to consider that many on this road will still be in the practice stage. They may not have a capital "L" (Learner, not Loser!) stuck on their backs, but we can see the struggle. Therefore, people, a little compassion and patience goes a long way!

If that's too difficult, think of everyone as a member of your own family. Makes a difference, doesn't it?

Let's keep that in mind as we go down the road on the way to the party!

On the Way to the Party
GREAT EXPECTATIONS

We all do it, and it's really quite a normal part of life. We enter the world expecting that when we cry, someone will be there to fill one end and empty the other. We grow up expecting to have several meals a day, a place to live (be it in the projects or a palace), and support for anything we choose to undertake. We go off to school, and even that's an expectation. And so it goes through all of life's stages.

There's nothing innately wrong with expecting certain things to happen in a given order; however, when these expectations don't bring the desired results, what happens to our emotions? Without getting too deep into the psychology of it, hurt wants to creep in, judgements against the person who failed me, criticism, and resentment want to take up permanent residency. Now I'm not a psychologist … I'm merely a human who has at times experienced unmet expectations, and it stinks.

Would it be better if I disciplined myself to no longer expect anything of anyone? I can't imagine what a relationship would be like if that were the case! There are many times and certain situations in which it's entirely acceptable to expect certain things. There are also those times when we should communicate our expectation to the other person involved; after all, they're not mind readers. For example, when my children were young, it was fine for them to expect that I would feed them breakfast before they went to school in the morning. In fact, I expected that of myself! But if they wanted to go to a friend's house after school and needed me to pick them up, they would need to communicate that to me. How could I know otherwise?

I look at many people and see pain and anger because of unmet expectations, and with that comes broken relationships. Husband and wife, parent and child, friends and business partners all suffering because something they thought should have been done one way, wasn't. No matter that the end result was probably the same. And even if it wasn't … Sometimes we wrongly have specific expectations and will almost certainly be disappointed, and that's possibly more of a control issue.

I'm speaking to myself more than anyone today, because I see this as something of a personal challenge, and it has been on my mind a lot lately! Not everyone will always do or be what I need them to do or be. In those cases, I need to examine my own heart. Did I expect something that they were incapable of giving? Or maybe the time just wasn't right, and my wish went unfulfilled. Time to dig out forgiveness and keep going forward! Time to affirm love and confidence in the other and become more sensitive to others' situations! Maybe it's also time to think about sharpening those communication skills. After all, what do you expect?

Expecting and fulfilling others' expectations is what makes the world go 'round. Don't stop. Do stop expecting unfairly and then building a wall out of hurt.

Right now I expect I have said enough and will just get on my way to the party!

On the Way to the Party
WHAT'S THAT SMELL?

I don't feel like doing this right now! There are a hundred things I'd rather be doing, especially since I've just come face to face with my own natural instincts *again*! It reminds me of something that happened about a year ago. It seemed that every time I opened the fridge, an unpleasant odour lingered faintly in the kitchen. I tried to ignore it, hoping it would just go away, all the while wondering what it could possibly be. Eventually the stench permeated the whole kitchen, and I tried to avoid opening the refrigerator any more than I absolutely had to. There's a weight loss plan for you—forget about the broccoli you bought three weeks ago and see how that works for you! It was time to do some serious investigating, yet I stalled. It wasn't until I walked into the house one day and realized it had moved in and taken over the whole place that I got serious about it. *This means war!* I thought as I marched over to the fridge and started pulling food off the shelves.

Some time later, I found it cowering in the back corner behind the romaine. If you have ever forgotten about those little green trees in there for a few weeks, you know what I'm talking about!

What I'm really talking about are attitudes and other less-than-pretty things in my life. Every once in a while, I get reminded of some ridiculous habit I have, or a stinky attitude I just displayed. Sometimes thoughts pop up, and instead of taking them captive, as scripture directs, I allow them to marinate in my brain for a while. Soon I sense a stench hanging on to me, and before long, I realize it's following me everywhere, and others are noticing! Just like my fridge, if I let little things like attitudes and wrong habits dictate my day, the stench will cling and grow and waft. Before long, everything about my life is contaminated.

So what to do? As I mentioned before, God's Word talks about taking every thought captive. Chain it up and toss it out! Don't dwell on it if it's not a worthy thought. Bad habits can be broken, but only if they're replaced with a positive action to reinforce a good habit. As a child of God, I am challenged in His Word to live in the presence of Jesus, and that will bring a sweet fragrance with it (2 Corinthians 2:15).

Every once in a while, it's a good idea to open myself up to an honest heart-searching and take out those things that are starting to rot and spoil. I need to sift through what needs to go and get rid of it immediately. That awful smell will dissipate, and a sweetness will fill the atmosphere as sure as the sun will shine again after the rain!

I think I learned my lesson as far as my refrigerator is concerned. That's the easier one to learn, Now for the rest. It seems like a lifelong task, and I pray that I'll be as patient with others on the journey as I'd like them to be with me.

After all, we'd rather be smelling the scent of roses on the way to the party!

On the Way to the Party
YOU HOLD THE KEY

The struggle lasted for many years … more than half my life by the time I found my way out. As a young child, I believed that my life was entirely normal, and that every girl grew up that way. The older I got and the more aware I became, I realized that my normal was not normal for everyone. That's when the pain and shame set in, settling deeper and deeper over time. Then one day I realized that I was unique, and no one else would understand. How wrong was that thought!

After stuffing pain for years, a sort of paralysis set in, and I felt like an emotional cripple. Still believing the lie that no one would be able to relate and understand, I let the pain sink into my depths until it became one with me. I became incapable of feeling anything.

When my children came along, I just wanted to be a loving mother and give them all the affection and emotional support they needed—all that I had craved as a child. Unfortunately, I felt at a loss, since I felt so incapable and empty. I began to cry out to God and ask Him to take away the pain so that I could be all I needed to be for my children. Do you believe God hears and answers? I have no doubt He heard me that time, and many more times after that!

This began a journey of significance for me; it seemed that every time I picked up a magazine and read an article, it spoke to my problem and answered a question that was burning in me at the time. Every time I was introduced to a new book, it seemed to point right to my need and address my personal issues. I'd be watching television, and a talk show or documentary would deal with whatever was troubling me.

During that time a battle was raging inside of me: Should I talk about it with a trusted person and lighten the load, or should I keep my mouth shut and allow the pressure to build and inevitably blow! My family stood by and loved me unconditionally, although I made it a daily challenge for them. This simply served as a reminder of how my heavenly Father pours His unconditional love on me, and I was humbled by it!

One amazing day when the feelings of hopelessness were almost overwhelming, I "accidentally" flipped to a channel where someone was talking about the need to forgive those who have hurt us. No, you don't need to wait for an apology or request for forgiveness. You don't even have to feel like forgiving the perpetrator(s). It's a choice you make, and then you act on it! In no way is this condoning any wrong committed against you, but it frees the person doing the forgiving.

This was not an entirely new concept for me, having heard it preached and taught many times. However, this time my heart was ready, willing, and able to make that choice. In a very physical manner, I went about burying the proverbial hatchet as the speaker stated repeatedly, "You hold the key to your own freedom."

I can't describe the sensation of being released within myself, and my life has shown the full result since then. I AM FREE! Nothing can ever convince me otherwise. I read in the Bible where Jesus Himself said that whoever the Son sets free is free indeed (John 8:36). I have no doubt that God heard my desperate plea and sent all I needed into my life at just the right time, gently leading me to the place where I was ready to make the right choice when faced with a decision. Now I just want others in the midst of a similar struggle to see victory in their lives and experience the fullness of joy that comes when we live a life free from constant, gnawing pain and the anger it brings. Use that key, unlock your heart, and forgive! Freedom is yours!

So now joy keeps me bubbling along on my way to the party!

On the Way to the Party
WHILE THE WORLD WATCHED
AND WAITED …

... *a*nd then heaved a collective sigh of relief and deep satisfaction. I don't have the words to describe the helplessness and hopelessness I felt upon hearing of thirteen young men trapped in a cave in Thailand. They were literally held captive by rising, murky water and blackness so thick it was palpable. They could only hang on to a thread of hope that they'd be found in time. The narrow ledge that served as their home for over two weeks could easily have become their tomb.

But that didn't happen! The moment word went out that they were missing, many stepped up to offer their knowledge, wisdom, and expertise. Without the involvement of total strangers, I fear that the result would have been sadly different. Members of the search and rescue team knew that they could also lose their own lives, but something drove them on. As I watched the most recent broadcast of *20/20*, I heard many express that this was by far the most difficult dive they'd ever undertaken.

So why did they do it? When I think of my six grandsons, who are around the same age as the trapped boys, my heart aches for the families that lived the terror of the ordeal. I know I would do whatever I could to help—anything at all. Across the ocean from where all the action was taking place, all I could do was pray and believe that they were in God's care and that He would bring them out! I know that countless other people were doing the same thing. This unity in prayer opened the way for a miracle to be manifested. Not only were the boys found against all odds, but against much greater odds, everyone came out of the cave alive and without major injuries! The supernatural strength that must have carried the rescuers astounds me. And in the face of the already most difficult task, they lost, not one, but two of their own! Yet they kept going with an out-of-this world determination that no more lives would be lost on their watch.

To aid in the rescue, powerful pumps were put in place to reduce the amount of water in the cave channels. After the team was safely out of the cave, but before all the members of the rescue team had exited, the pumps failed and torrents of water immediately rushed the men as they struggled to remove the last of the equipment. They all made it out safely, because no one gave up! What a lesson for us when we so often wimp out on little issues and are tempted to run away, pout, and feel sorry for ourselves.

As I look around me, I determine that with all I've got going for me, I will do what I can to help those who walk this path beside me and run into difficult times. I renew my resolve to be grateful for all my blessings. Although I've never received a "big" miracle like this, many miracles make up my everyday. I'm so thankful to God for bringing me through a lot of stuff that had me sitting on my own little ledge in the dark and feeling utterly helpless! Just like in the parable Jesus told of the shepherd leaving the many in the safety of the fold to search for the one lost sheep, God still searches for and rescues those whom He loves and longs to have a relationship with!

So I keep my eyes open for those that need a rescuing touch on the way to the party!

On the Way to the Party
SO THIS IS FAMILY!

Well, here we are at the long-awaited reunion. This is the fifth one, the other four being held while our parents were still in attendance! Now that generation has all passed on, and after a nineteen-year hiatus, it is *time*! How fortunate that about forty of the cousins are able to gather and compare notes, aka brag, about our grandchildren. It's all good. It's what we do best!

Okay, so we look a little older, have added a few more pounds, walk a little slower, and start a story but forget the punchline. We're all from the same tree and share the same roots, so we get it!

Being family doesn't mean we're the same or share the same ideas and opinions all the time. It *does* mean that we accept each other in our differences and love and care for each other in spite of them. When one hurts, we all hurt. When one succeeds, we all celebrate! When one is missing, we feel fragmented.

Come to think of it, family was God's idea in the first place. In scripture He calls Himself our Father, and He calls us His children. In 1 John 3:18, John refers to followers of Christ as "*little children*," encouraging them to not just love with words but with actions and in truth. I like that! It reminds me that words are not enough. Genuine love needs to be relayed with actions. And then it calls me to love and to begin with those closest to me. My family. I never chose them, but I choose to love them and accept them just as they are. And hopefully they will love and accept me as I am. As God loves and accepts all of us!

I look forward to another reunion, when we will never have to part again! In the meantime, I continue on the way to the party.

On the Way to the Party
JUST LIKE DADDY

We all have at least one; some are good and kind and wonderful, others not so much. Some create memories that leave us with the warm fuzzies, while, if I'm going to be honest, others leave us cold with the shakes and shivers. Yes, I speak of fathers. At some point, every little boy wants to be like him, and every little girl wants to belong to him.

I'm reminded of a time ten years ago when I travelled to another province to be on hand for the birth of my grandson. My daughter already had a two-year-old, and we quite enjoyed the show this little guy put on for us from time to time! When there was talk of us going somewhere, be it grocery shopping, a trip to the beach, or simply a walk to the local playground, he would immediately jump into action. We laughed as we watched him run all over the house, looking under chairs and the couch, opening drawers, and rummaging in the toy box. All the while he was chattering, "My pone, my teyth, my pone, my teyth!" For those of you not accustomed to toddler-speak, I will translate: "My phone, my keys, my phone, my keys!"

We found it so funny because at least once a day we watched the older version, aka Daddy, doing the same thing! Max had inherited his dad's old cellphone and a key ring with various keys attached to it.

These had become his favourite toys. Of course, Daddy couldn't leave the house without these basic necessities; therefore, neither could Max.

As cute as it was, it drove home the point that we want and need someone to emulate. There's something inside of us that desires to be just like Daddy!

We read in 1 John 3:2: "*Beloved, we are God's children now, and what we will be has not yet appeared; but we know that when he appears we shall be like him, because we shall see him as he is*" (ESV). I hang on to this promise as I walk the journey called life. Those days when nothing goes right, when everything seems to line up against me, the times when sadness settles in and seems in no hurry to leave … I hang on with a soul-sustaining grip. Those days I *know* that one day I will see Him and be like Him, all strength and no weakness, all love and no insecurities!

As I travel this path, I must remember to take my "pone and my teyth," because I never know when I might need them on the way to the party!

On the Way to the Party
AFTER THE STORM

Have you ever stood by an open window and just breathed deeply of the fresh, rain-scented air after a summer rain storm? If not, it should be on your bucket list. Just this evening, for instance, I was standing at my kitchen sink and finishing up the supper dishes. The window in front of me was open, and after a couple of days of incessant heat, the cool, fresh breeze nearly caused me to swoon! It had been raining off and on all day and had brought a good measure of relief. Now the fresh air felt as good as it smelled!

It brought to mind another summer eight years ago when there was no relief from the storm. We were battered day after day, the black clouds hanging low against a backdrop of gun-metal grey. No sooner did the heavy, dark blankets of cloud begin to move off than more rolled in, heavier and more ominous than the ones before. No, I'm not talking about the kind that shed their moisture and move on. Rather, I'm referring to the emotional state of mind our family experienced during that season of our lives. My husband was extremely ill, and the prognosis was not good. Every day was like a roller coaster ride: first hearing a promising report, then two hours later having our hopes dashed *again*! The one constant was our faith in a living God who was walking through the storm with us and would eventually bring back the sunshine after the rain.

When my husband graduated to his eternal home, the thunder and lightning shattered the peace again … for a time. I wondered if I would ever experience joy again, and I seriously doubted it. But then my mind and heart began to focus, by choice, on the promise of an omnipresent God who said He would never leave me. He promised to walk by my side through the valley of the shadow of death, according to Psalm 23. The more captivated I was by the promises of God, the less I focussed on my sadness and loneliness. Life began to look brighter and fresher as the days went on. Joy and peace returned; the big storm was over, and a fresh breeze brought the relief I'd been longing for!

Now as I move along in my journey, storms still threaten to overtake from time to time, but I face them with the assurance that they will not stick around for long and most certainly will not control my life. The sun will shine again after the storm, and I will just continue on my way to the party!

On the Way to the Party
THROUGH THE SMOKE

I've got to do it. I can't stop myself; it's like an addiction! Yes, I confess I love watching sunsets, even if I can just catch the slightest glimpse. I've lived in many different locations and seen the most beautiful, breathtaking sunsets from every angle imaginable, yet each time is like witnessing a visual miracle new and fresh!

In the last couple of weeks, I've had mixed feelings about it, though. I look toward the west, and the haze and smoke create a unique glow as the sun begins to sink as if with the heaviness of the air. It carries a beauty of sorts yet reflects the heartache and hopelessness so many are currently experiencing.

So much loss and destruction have occurred to the west and south of us, yet we go on as if all was right with the world—until it touches us personally. I thank my God that we're not in imminent danger, yet things could shift quickly and unexpectedly. In the meantime, I give thanks that we're safe, and I pray a prayer of protection for those in the path of the raging flames, and those desperately fighting to assuage them.

Tonight I again observed the sun sink lower and lower to the horizon. As it descended into the hovering smoke covering the earth, the colour intensified until it was a bright red orb, like one giant tail light in the sky. If it weren't for the smoke cover, the bright ball in the sky wouldn't adopt that clear, red hue with the distinctly sharp edges. Almost speechless, it hit me: God's love is like that. It shines on us all the time, and we take it for granted. Good things happen, and we go on our merry way. Bad things happen, and we blame God. But still He showers us with rays of love. Challenges and difficulties come, and the more they seem to settle down on us, the more intensely we sense His love focused directly on us. Instead of being eclipsed by our hardships, we see His goodness and faithfulness more clearly. The night may fall, but we know that as we sit in darkness, His love shines on someone else, and come morning, we'll experience the warmth of His love in our lives again.

My dear friend, God's Word tells us: "*Weeping may endure for a night, but joy comes in the morning*" (Psalm 30:5b). This is not a suggestion or a cliché; it is a *promise*, and one that I cling to as I continue on the way to the party

On the Way to the Party
FIND THAT JEWEL

First, we made the choice to go, and then we bought the tickets online. Still, we had no idea where exactly this place was. After all was said and done, we googled "Rosebud." Imagine our surprise when we found that it was a tiny hamlet with less than one hundred permanent residents and less than fifty homes, yet it was boasted to be a major tourist attraction in southern Alberta.

Well, there's nothing like going there and checking it out. After an hour's drive, we headed down into a valley, and there it was! Looking very much like an old western movie set, it shone like a fine gem in the midst of the prairie badlands.

Needless to say, we thoroughly enjoyed our day—the dinner and live theatre, the shops, the unique attractions, and the art galleries. In fact, I believe I could visit again, check into one of their cozy bed and breakfast locations, and spend a few days exploring! What was impressed on me through this entire experience was that if we had never looked past the first tiny snippet of information, I would have missed one of the richest and most enjoyable experiences of my life.

I wonder how many times I've written off another person simply because the first, hurried impression didn't look all that interesting? In all honesty, if a little more time and interest are invested, we may find a treasure deep inside just waiting to be mined! There's no short cut to getting to really know a person. I know from experience that, in most cases, it's worth putting in the extra effort. I ask you to dig deep; don't write someone off because they look a little different, dress differently, or hold different views on certain subjects.

As for me, I plan to find all the treasures I can along the road as I continue on the way to the party!

On the Way to the Party
'TILL LATER

So my whole day was spent running an obstacle course in my own home, trying not to trip over sleeping bags, suitcases, and backpacks that looked a lot like I feel after a big Thanksgiving dinner—overstuffed, to say the least! As I oh so carefully made my way around the living room, as if walking through a minefield, I desperately tried to keep my mind off what had to transpire before the day was done.

They'd arrived last Thursday night ... with plans! Our trip to the zoo on Friday had me watching them watch the animals and loving every minute of it! I would have never imagined myself walking into some of the stores I ended up in, but oh what fun! And because I had another commitment on Saturday, they went to a movie on their own. This was new territory for me. I've never had a visit from three teenage grandchildren before, without their parents, but I loved every minute of our time together!

Now I sit here on the verge of tears, so please indulge an old lady for a few minutes. I delivered them to the camp bus on Sunday, and four days later, after too much silence, picked them up again. More running about for another day, and then it was time for the dreaded trip to the airport.

Now it seems that the house echoes in the silence, and I think I hear the sounds of *Animal Planet*, but upon checking, it's only the news. I can walk through the living room now and know the way will be clear. I open the refrigerator and know that the same jug of milk will still be there next week. In the same vein, when I open the pantry door, I know the Doritos are all gone and will need replenishing!

There's just something special about grandkids. When I look at them, I see how they're replicas of their parents, who are replicas of their parents, and so on. And suddenly it hits me … as long as life continues on this planet, I will be there in my own children and in their children and so on for generations to come. This challenges me to make my life and influence count.

Those kids are everything to me. I love them with all my heart and am so thankful for all eighteen of my grandchildren. Each one enriches my life in a way I could never have imagined! So tonight, after saying goodbye to three of them after having had close contact for a week, I was in tears as I left the airport and drove toward home. I know I'll see them again. I have the hope and confidence that I'll see them, if not here on earth, in our eternal home. And the truth is, some days I can't wait to get there.

As one of my grandsons said to his mom at the age of three when his home was under renovation: "I don't want to be heah. I'm going to Gwamma's house." And he came! Luckily, they lived only a few doors away!

Now when sadness and loneliness begin to weigh me down, I want to say, "I don't want to be heah. I'm going to God's house." God in His wisdom gives the grace to push through, and He walks the minefields of life with me. And at the right time—His time—I'll go to His house and see all those I have lost and will lose in this world. In the meantime, I walk on, move ahead, and continue to say hello and goodbye to many that I love.

After all, it's not really "goodbye" but just "'till later." In the meantime, I continue on my way to the party!

On the Way to the Party
HANG ON FOR DEAR LIFE!

I was so excited! I was hardly able to finish my breakfast, just putting in time 'till she said the magic word. *Finally*. I perked up my four-year-old ears as I heard my mom.

"Okay, you can go now."

My brother, almost six at the time, was to be my trusty escort all the way down the street to the town's single tiny general store at the end of the block. We set out on our journey, more incredible to me than *the* incredible journey. I'd never made this trip on my own before—that is, without my mother or a much older sibling. My "grocery" list consisted of one item: a big, yellow, shiny bubble gumball. I don't quite recall, but I believe I may have even been salivating at the thought of biting into that minty morsel!

I close my eyes now and allow myself to go back there; the smell of diesel, or whatever fuel used in trains sixty-two years ago, was sharp … so sharp that it stung my nose a bit. The clanging of heavy metal (no, not a rock band) followed us as we walked down the street, which ran parallel to the railway track. My expense account, a penny, brought a damp itch to the sweaty palm of my right hand. The fact that it was mid-April and the street wasn't paved but rather a channel of sticky gumbo was of little concern, as my thoughts were focused on the prize ahead! Little did I know! The storefront popped into sight, and my feet tried to move faster, but the gumbo prevented them.

Suddenly, we had arrived. It didn't take long for me to make my purchase, and with my brother having made his choice as well, we left the building and headed for home. I'm sure we tried to walk a little faster on the return trip, and that may be what landed us in trouble. As we approached our house, I went to take a step … and walked right out of my little rubber boot! With my foot covered in the sticky, brownish clay, I turned around and tried to unstick my boot. As I fought to free it, the other boot got caught in the same trap, and now I was standing mid-calf in the gooey gumbo!

By this time, my brother had gone home and alerted my mother, who came to my rescue. I suppose she was able to save my boots, but I went home in muddy stockings that were now about ten inches too long at the toes! Do you want to know what was the most amazing thing about my adventure? I never once let go of my bubble gum! No siree! I hung on for dear life, because I knew how good it was; in fact, I could already taste it. I was crying, the tears mixing with the mud. My heart was breaking because I thought I'd lost my boots forever, as I was unable to pry them out of the mud one-handedly. But by gum, if anything was to stay behind, it would not be my gumball!

In my Bible I read an invitation to everyone. Psalm 34:8 says, "*Taste and see that the Lord is good; blessed is the one who takes refuge in him*" (NIV). I have tasted and seen many times over the course of many years that nothing compares to His goodness as I let Him hide me in the middle of a storm, and I've been through a few. I'm saddened when I see people let go of their faith or their desire to walk with God when hard times come and they need Him the most. Taste and see! That's all He asks.

Just like a little four-year-old girl walked down that muddy street and lost her boots, caking her stockings with the gross, sticky stuff but never letting go of the real treasure, hang on to Jesus when things go well and when life gets hard. He promises refuge to those who trust in Him;

just hang on for dear life. One of these days I'll arrive at the party, and I'm committed to hang on to the treasure all the way.

As for now, I grip that promise and hang on for dear life on my way to the party!

On the Way to the Party
JUST EXCHANGE IT!

There I sat, Sunday morning, and I was dressed in my prettiest dress, my hair all kinked up from having been done up in paper curls the night before. Everyone else was rushing around doing their last-minute prep before piling into the old Ford and heading to church. No one really had a moment for little ol' me, but then the brain of a four-year-old is rarely out of great ideas! Then it hit me! Why not go next door and play with Lisa while I waited? Not only was she my dad's boss's daughter, but she was also my best friend and sometimes partner in crime!

I left the house quietly and made my way next door. I knocked on the screen door and then waited a long time. It must have been all of one and a half minutes. No answer, so I tried the door. It was unlocked, sooo … I entered the porch and proceeded to knock on the inside door. In the meantime, my eyes landed on the boxes of freshly picked peas sitting on the bench. I decided to change course slightly and grabbed a handful before making a quick exit.

Back at home, I sat on the steps and began enjoying my new-found treat—that is, until my dad came out to start the car. He very quickly got to the bottom of it, and I simply could not lie. The truth came tumbling out, and one very unhappy little girl was marched right back to the neighbours. The lady of the house actually answered the door, much to my disappointment, and a heartfelt apology was given.

I've never forgotten what happened next, as it has been re-played and reinforced in many different scenarios throughout the more than six decades since. When I handed her the little handful of peas, half of which were mouldy anyway, she excused herself for a moment. She returned with a small container of fresh raspberries and a smile, telling me how much she appreciated my honesty and the return of the peas!

Actually, that very same thing has happened to me many times in my life. Oh no, I no longer go around stealing peas from people's porches. But there have been times when I felt stuck with something that was not so pleasant to deal with. Habits have been developed—you know, those pesky little things that can cause havoc in your relationships, work life, and other areas.

I've learned that there is Someone I can go to, and then hand to Him my smelly attitudes, resentments, and hurt feelings. When I give them to Jesus, He gives me something else in return. I can imagine Him smiling as He pours His love, joy, and peace out on me. No matter what my day has been like, when I stand before my God, all broken up and in pain, I know that the hurt stops there, because His strength is enough for me, and He freely gives me all the good He has promised. But I must free my hands of the stuff that brings me only pain and make room to hold all the wonderful things He has for me. Fulfillment in life, purpose, and direction are mine, and with my container full of goodies, I go along on my way to the party!

On the Way to the Party
AND ALONG CAME WORK …

D o you ever get the feeling that you'd like just a teeny bit of spice added to your life? I can honestly say that throughout my adult life, there have been countless times when life was going so well, I felt I had it all: a loving husband, great kids, awesome friendships, a church family, involvement that I found absolutely fulfilling, and so much more. Yet at times I'd feel an underlying tug toward "something" that would put a little extra *zing!* in my life. I wasn't bored, and I always felt I had the best life had to offer.

Moving through life, I eventually discovered that this impression would assail me just before a bend in the road! For example, a certain emptiness was pushing at me when suddenly we found ourselves in a place where we were able to be of assistance to people who were trying desperately to escape a local communal cult. Although there were many ups and downs and bumps in the road, there was a deep, unfettered joy and fulfillment in knowing we were available to someone reaching out for help.

Then there was the time we were asked if we'd be interested in taking in a foreign exchange student for the school year. We agreed, she came, and we spent the first month struggling to communicate, since she knew very little English, and we much less French! The rewards of that year far outweighed the challenges, and we put her on the plane ten months later with breaking hearts as we bid our "daughter" farewell.

So here I am again, much water having flowed under the bridge. For the past four years I've been enjoying a new phase of life. My family more than doubled a few years back, and after a couple of moves I had a new community and church to adapt to. And in it creeps …

For a few years now, having struggled with some health issues and ensuing surgeries, I truly felt my "working" days were over. Then out of the blue an opportunity was practically dumped in my lap, and I knew instantly: *This is it. It's a perfect fit for me!*

The job is temporary, lasting two weeks, but with the option that it may be offered several times a year. Only three hours a day. I think I can handle that, and the people I work with are amazing, both the supervisors and my co-workers. Basically, if you can count and know how to hold a pencil correctly, you can handle the work. It gets me out and about in the morning and puts me in a place where I have to be awake, alert, and accurate—just enough challenge without being overwhelming and stressful. Perfect for this lady, I say!

I've learned in life that when I'm walking along and enjoying my relationship with my creator God, there may be times when this restlessness hits. As I submit to the Lord of my life, He always leads me down a new path to complete happiness and fulfilling joy. My prayer is that as I walk along, I'll be able to help others along this path and bring a touch of love and comfort when needed, an encouraging smile, or a wee word of wisdom! That's all I ask as I continue on my way to the party.

On the Way to the Party
GROW UP, ALREADY!

Has anyone ever told you to grow up? Come on, be honest … I know I've said that to my kids a time or two, and they did!

Somehow things just magically change. As a child, whenever I was asked how old I was, I would stand as tall as I could (which wasn't that much, since as an adult I never reached more than five feet two and a half inches) and proudly declare my age: "six and a half" or "seven and three quarters."

Now as a "mature" adult, I reply with "sixty-five," even if my sixty-sixth birthday is tomorrow (gulp)! Okay, smarty pants, so where is the seven-sixteenth, or whatever, now?

My heart still smiles as I remember a trip I took to the beautiful province of Newfoundland seven years ago. I had recently lost my husband, and my daughter invited me to join them in Manitoba for the summer. They were expecting a new baby and could use the moral support as well as a few extra hands. During my stay, we flew to my son-in-law's home province to attend his sister's wedding, as well as show off the new grandson!

On the first leg of our flight, my little grandson, Max, barely five at the time, excitedly announced, "This is my first plane ride when I'm big!" Of course we understood that he meant that he knew he had flown before but simply had no memory of it.

Oh, how we long to grow up so fast, yet there are so many things we don't particularly like about being grown up: responsibility, accountability, bills, or practising self- control. That last one is truly a hurdle for me, and I seem to trip on it every time I make a run for it!

I've recently become part of a group that's helping me take a real, honest look at *me* and understand some of my issues. Hopefully I'll be able to improve my ability to see the truth and kick denial to the curb. No, it's not everyone else who has problems; I have them too! According to Psalm 139, the God who made me and wrote the book about my life also has a purpose and plan for me (Jeremiah 29:11). He has even prepared all the good works that He has purposed me for (Ephesians 2:10); therefore, I have no excuse. God desires for me to "grow up" and fulfill the task before me to bring glory to Him and no other. And for this He gives me new mercies and opportunities every day, and He forgives my sins and failures of the day before. Knowing this, I look forward to growing and maturing on my way to the party!

On the Way to the Party
HERO OR ZERO?

It was a beautiful Saturday morning. Bright sunshine and clear, crisp air enveloped us as we made our way west. Our trip from Winnipeg, Manitoba to Edmonton, Alberta had been prompted by the need to have our daughter visit a specialist there. As a busy mom, I was just happy for the change of scenery and a chance for family bonding, which I was sure would be accomplished by enforced togetherness!

A few hours into the drive, frustration was beginning to set in. Oh, the kids were doing well in the back seat, and no fights had broken out, but we kept making what I saw as silly, unnecessary stops. Such time wasters! It wasn't until later in the day that we realized that for things to work out as they did, timing was everything!

Being September 25, the air was on the cool side but nice enough for a picnic. We had planned on taking a little side trip to Souris, a town in Manitoba known for its swinging bridge across the river. We planned on stopping in the park for a picnic lunch before attempting a walk on the bridge.

We had just taken our seats and were ready to enjoy the rest of our day when we saw a tiny girl running toward our table. She stopped and, while panting for breath, told us that her little brother had fallen into the river and couldn't swim.

We immediately jumped into action. My husband, Larry Heppner, took off for the river. I took the car and went to the nearest store to call 911, and we instructed our girls to stay put and pray!

Eventually the ambulance and police arrived, by which time Larry had already dived into the ice-cold water three times. After the second try, he was standing on the dock and trying to assess if he had the stamina to make another attempt. By this time, the child had been in the river for at least twenty minutes. As he was deciding whether to try again or walk away, he heard the voice of an older child say urgently, "Try one more time!" We found out later that an eleven-year-old boy was standing at the edge of the woods and had witnessed the whole thing. My husband said that was all the encouragement he needed. As a result of that little prompt, he tried again, and when the emergency team arrived, he had the little boy on the dock and had begun administering CPR!

The little face began to pink up as water spewed from his mouth. At this point, the medical personnel took over, and in a few minutes the boy was on his way to the hospital. Shock now set in for Larry as his entire body began to shake uncontrollably. The police insisted he get checked out in the hospital, so they took him, and I followed with my girls in our car. I began to realize how easily we could have lost him to hypothermia or any number of related complications.

After some time, we were on our way again, thanking God for sparing the life of a dear little boy and saving our husband and daddy from harm! Oh yes, and the timing? As it was, we were the only people brave enough to face the chill in the air and have a picnic on a crisp sunny day near the end of September. Were it not for all the "unnecessary" stops, we wouldn't have been there at the right time. How blessed we felt that God would use us to save a life!

We continued to marvel at the goodness and faithfulness of our loving heavenly Father! That day twenty-five years ago, my husband was branded a hero by one little boy and his family. Some time later, one of our daughters wrote a school report titled "My Dad, My Hero." Larry only did what he knew he had to do, just like many of you. We won't all be called on to rescue a drowning child, but we are all called to be a hero and fill a particular need in someone's life. Maybe the need is a word of encouragement to the one who is closer to a given situation, but in any case, we are all called, and someone needs us to get involved.

What about you? Do you know someone who needs you to be their hero? Will you say yes, or will you run the other way because you don't want to get involved? Will you be a hero, or a zero?

I know I want to be one who helps and encourages anyone I meet on the way to the party!

On the Way to the Party
LOG OUT

O kay, so anyone who knows me knows that I'm a few sandwiches short of a picnic when it comes to technology! Just to prove my point, it's been a year since I joined Facebook, and it's taken me that long to figure out what "log out" means.

After reading a year's worth of comments, some of which are snarky, ignorant, and even downright rude, I'm beginning to get the picture. We call them "friends," yet I'm not so sure a true friend would respond with some of the remarks I've had the "pleasure" of reading. Makes me wish everyone would just log out. Now before all my friends in Facebook-land start hurling verbal stones, let me explain. I have *finally* figured out what "log out" means!

Recently as I was reading my Bible, I came across a lesson taught by Jesus in His famous sermon on the mount. As recorded in Mathew 7:3–5, Jesus, speaking to His followers, tells them to take the log out of their own eye before attempting to remove a speck in someone else's eye. Seems basic common sense to me. How can one see clearly with a tree limb jutting out of one's eye? And then try to remove a speck of sawdust out of his brother's eye? I can imagine Jesus having a little fun with this one, holding a large stick up to His eye to illustrate!

Please understand that I'm not commenting on my friends or the replies I get personally. You guys are all amazing, uplifting, and encouraging, as friends should be. In fact, just thinking of this challenges me to look for the best in others, because I know that what I seek and focus on is what I see and how I interpret. That's difficult for me at times. My daughter once challenged me to look for and believe the best of others in a given situation. How did she ever get so smart?

So now I have to continually remind myself to take the "log out" of my own eye before I "speck"ulate on someone else's mistakes, or what I perceive to be their bad! Come to think of it, it also clears my vision so I can proceed safely on the way to the party!

On the Way to the Party

MY DISAPPOINTMENT, HIS APPOINTMENT

Have you ever been in the place where you were intensely looking forward to something and suddenly it was whisked out of your hands, and there was nothing you could do about it? A few days ago, I was travelling to visit my children and grandchildren. As usual when I make this trek across the prairie provinces, I had my favourite music blaring and was singing along gustily (if that's even a word) when I began to recognize a few landmarks and suddenly realized where I was.

The memories began to scroll through my mind. *There's where I started my first marriage, right near that First Nations community.* I remembered some of the lovely people we got to know, and that led me to another memory, a much more recent one.

Two years ago, I was finished my autumn visit to Manitoba and had begun the return trip home. I was planning a short overnight visit to my sister's house. The next day after an early departure I would stop in at the home of a dear friend for breakfast. Our friendship dated back to high school, but we had only recently found each other after many years.

Before arriving at my sister's, I got a phone call from my long-lost friend. She told me that she had made a mistake in thinking their flight to a cruise destination was leaving a day later than it actually was.

Therefore, she had to cancel our rendezvous, as they would be boarding the plane about the same time I was to arrive at their house.

The disappointment was intense for a moment, but I know that sometimes things don't work out exactly as I plan them, but God often has a detour plan for me, and He doesn't make mistakes. I prayed a quick prayer, asking, "God, is there something else you want me to do? Someone else you want me to meet?"

Just as I finished praying, the thought came to me: I should drive past my friend's house and take the highway through the First Nations reservation where we lived so many years ago. And of course, while there I should try to locate Leroy and Jessie. I didn't even remember their last name. Complete peace and contentment flooded me at that point.

The following morning, I left as planned and took the route through the reserve. Arriving at the core of the settlement, I stopped at a gas station that offered a cafe as well. Behind the counter sat a young lady, and to the side stood an older woman, a few years older than myself. I gave my name and explained that my husband and I had lived there and ran a Sunday school in the home of Leroy and Jessie. Did she happen to know where I could find this couple now, if they still lived there?

The girl gave me a funny look and pointed to the more mature lady beside her, who then said, "I'm Jessie!"

I couldn't believe it! It turned out that she worked there part time. This was a large reserve, so coincidence? I don't think so! After sharing for a while over a cup of coffee, I left her with one of my newly published books. The story of her life and several losses of family members had left her feeling rather raw and pain-filled. I prayed that her spirits had been lifted a little by my visit and the hope-filled words I spoke.

It's not always that clear, but God has a plan for every one of His children, and when we actually want to hear from Him, He takes us at our word. Sometimes He adds a little twist to our day, and always with good purpose! Now when my plans are suddenly re-routed, I don't panic; I know there's a plan in play that is much bigger than me and much farther reaching than I can comprehend.

Friend, when your plans go awry, give it to God and trust Him to work out the details in a way only He can. Someone needs you … you just don't know it yet! The Bible tells us in Ephesians 2:10 that we are created for good works, which God has prepared in advance for us to do. He was there; He re-directed my path, put that lady on my mind, and then set her right in front of me. How much clearer can it get?

As I journey through this life, I don't look at failed plans as disappointments but as His appointments, and that keeps me going on the way to the party!

On the Way to the Party
KEEP RIGHT ON WALKING!

Have you ever just watched someone walk? Each of us has our own peculiar, unique way of walking. It's so much more than just putting one foot in front of the other to get from point A to B.

This past week I've had the privilege of picking up my three grandsons from their school. I always enjoy being the first one in the family to get that first-hand report on who ran faster than his buddy at recess, or who had the most sensible explanation for that all-important question, "Does the wind make the trees move, or does the trees' movement cause the wind to blow?" Then there's the other big one: "Why are some kids allergic to peanut butter, and others aren't?" Ah! There's nothing like an after-school discussion while riding in a car, and no one can escape while Grandma imparts her own special brand of wisdom!

Anyway, back to walking. As I'm sitting in the car and waiting for my boys to come out, I watch all the others pouring through the doors and making their way down the sidewalk. Even from a distance, I can tell that they aren't "my" boys. I've known and loved them from the moment I knew they were on the way, and that love only grew and intensified with their birth and their first couple of years in our family. Now after watching them navigate their world on their own two feet for many years, I know their walk. When they round the corner of their school and make their way down the sidewalk, I take note of their unique little bounce or swagger, and even from more than a block away, my heart takes a leap of pride as I think, *Those are my little guys!*

The desire of my heart is that when God looks at me, He will recognize from my walk that I belong to Him and His family, and that His heart will bulge with pride to call me His! In Ephesians 5:15, Paul says, "*Therefore be careful how you walk, not as unwise men but as wise*" (NASB). The "walk" here can be interchanged with the word "live."

So how is your walk? Can people look at the way you live and see that you are a wise, kind, loving person? Will God have good reason to look at your walk with pride and say, "Look at my kid! Isn't he (she) awesome?" I want my Father God to see me with the button bustin' pride I feel when I see my grandkids rounding the corner and recognize their little-man gait as they make their way to my car!

For that reason, I "walk" carefully as I make my way to the party!

On the Way to the Party
HOW ABOUT THAT ROADKILL?

So here I was, lead-footing it back to Calgary after two weeks away from home. I can't describe how wonderful it was to see my kids and grandkids who live so far from me! Everything wonderful begins with a dream and ends with another; this one ended with the dream of returning home.

I made a few stops on the way, extending them somewhat for a brief visit with friends. During the entire drive, though, I kept my eyes peeled for a glimpse of wildlife. The highlight of any road trip for me is viewing wild animals in their natural habitat, just doing what comes naturally and being the beautiful creatures God created them to be! I saw one coyote and all the usual birds, but nothing else. But wait! A large number of animals had, over the miles, met an untimely demise right there in the middle of the road.

As I continued to pile up the long miles behind me with nothing to do but think, I thought. I was reminded of how we can so easily sail through life without giving a thought to the wounded and hurting falling around us. To make it more personal, some may even fall under the power and influence of my hands or mouth. A momentary lapse in judgement on my part can cause great pain and suffering to another. A sharp word spoken thoughtlessly may bring me a moment of euphoric release but cause someone else's spirit to wither and die. My hard attitude toward someone in need of compassionate acceptance may be the difference between that person believing in a loving God or further hardening their heart. I made a re-commitment to "walk carefully" so that others can see clearly whose child I am and which family I belong to.

As I travel through life, I'd like to think that I leave a conversation or a chance meeting having infused a little life-giving positivity into a given situation. Everyone needs that; *no one* needs put-downs or jabs where it already hurts. Can you relate to this?

My new resolve is to see people who are created in the image of God begin to view themselves exactly as that. It's a well documented fact that when we have a revelation of who we are in Jesus Christ, we naturally act accordingly. I desire to be that person who brings others to that revelation, lifting them up instead of knocking them down. I wonder if I've been the cause of any "road kill" in the past. By the grace of God, I hope not!

As I continue my journey, I keep the eyes of my soul peeled and hopefully leave no roadkill on my way to the party.

On the Way to the Party
I LOVE MY TOES!

Not long ago, I saw my toes for the first time in about eight years! No, not because my belly got in the way! Due to an old injury, I had a torn tendon in my foot, which caused my arch to fall. Over the years without medical intervention, my right foot became extremely distorted and misshapen. Along with this came a lot of pain and difficulty in function as the years went by.

The previous October, I'd finally undergone reconstructive surgery. Before the operation, my surgeon had told me that at a subsequent time, after healing, he would have to do another surgery to straighten three or four toes on my right foot. Because of nerve damage caused by the original injury, the toes had curled under so badly, it was impossible to see the entire toe and nail. Instead, only tiny nubs were present to my view. Today my ankle and foot look quite normal, and I'm able to walk comfortably, free from pain. For this I thank God, who provided me with a wonderful, competent surgeon. He did an amazing job. Only my toes were still presenting a bit of a challenge. Balled up as they were, it was difficult to find comfortable shoes, and it also caused me a little pain.

I was scheduled to see my orthopaedic surgeon on Wednesday, October 31. The plan was to ask him about setting a date for the next surgery. I was not looking forward to having another interruption in my life, and I didn't want to go that route; therefore, I'd been asking the Great Physician to heal those toes and straighten them supernaturally. I'll admit it—I'm a wimp! I also know that my God is able to heal, and I want His name to be lifted up by whatever happens in my life!

One verse of scripture that came to my mind over the years whenever I got discouraged looking at my "ugly" foot was from Isaiah: "*How beautiful on the mountains are the feet of the messenger who brings good news, the good news of peace and salvation ...*" (Isaiah 52:7, NLT). As I would declare that verse over my foot, I'd determine again to be that messenger of peace and good news to whoever came into my life that day. In doing so, I also left the "problem" with the Great Problem Solver!

So there I was, on the night before my doctor's appointment. I took off my shoes and socks and happened to glance down at my feet and ... what was that looking up at me? There they were, my little pink toenails, whom I barely recognized! I hadn't seen them for so long, and just a few days earlier they had still been tightly curled! I screamed! I cried! I laughed! I shouted "Thank you, Jesus," recognizing it as nothing short of a miracle! I give the glory to God, knowing that it didn't "just happen." God showed me again that He has a plan for my life, and I guess right now it's not for me to spend the next six weeks sitting around while recovering from surgery!

The next day I saw my doctor, and he agreed that there was no need for straightening toes that were already straight. Every time I see them, I'm reminded of how "broken" they were and how beautiful they are now. Are you broken and in need of a miracle? The same God who cares enough about lowly little toes cares a whole lot about you! He wants to heal and complete your life. God is good!

Yes, I do love my toes and will continue walking on them all the way to the party!

On the Way to the Party
PERFECTLY AND PROPERLY PICKLED

Just the other day I opened a jar of home-canned dill pickled cucumbers. Yum! I could taste them already, even as I went about breaking the seal. I remembered the tangy blend of the salty sourness, the crispy crunch as I bit in, and the way my sinuses would clear as the tiny chunks slid down my throat! Moments later, we sat down to enjoy our dinner. I helped myself to a pickle and with utter horror realized that it did *not* match up with my previous experiences! Now, I've been pickling for over forty years and had never before come up with a product similar to this. What could have gone wrong?

I took another bite and tried to analyze. Eventually, I came to the conclusion that I must have forgotten the salt. There was definitely enough dill, garlic, and vinegar, even the faintly sweet edge added by the minuscule amount of sugar the recipe called for.

I remembered the day I made them, how I was just a tad rushed and had to cook up two separate batches of brine. The previously opened jars had produced pickles just as they should be, with proper proportions of vinegar, salt, garlic, and dill. Now I began to believe that one of the brine batches was definitely "sans sel" (and that, my friends, is the extent of my French). True horror set in as I remembered how I had proudly gifted many friends and family members with my efforts at home canning. If you're one of the lucky recipients, please know that this is simply a game of roulette: you may get a good jar, but on the other hand … So for all you unsuspecting loved ones, maybe you should refrain from trying the lovely looking UGOs (unidentified green objects)!

Seriously, though, it made me think about what Jesus said about salt. He actually called His followers *"the salt of the earth"* (Matthew 5:13). And then I began to wonder if I'm one of those people who adds a little flavour to the lives of those I meet, or am I one who should be *"thrown out and trampled underfoot"*?

Adding a tiny sprinkle of salt enhances the taste of just about anything. Sprinkling a little kindness, compassion, or well-doing can make life much more palatable for most people, not to mention the sense of joy and fulfillment it brings to the sprinkler.

What kind of person are you? Do you add a little flavour to the lives of those around you, or have you lost your saltiness? I believe Jesus likened us to salt so we would understand that when we touch people's lives for good, they will become thirsty for an experience with the One we follow. Then we can have the joy of leading them to Jesus, who has promised to give them a drink from the living water (Himself), and they will be forever satisfied!

As I walk this life path, I pray that I will always be reminded to spread a little salt wherever I go, 'till I arrive at the party.

On the Way to the Party
AND THE PARTY'S ON!

As you sit down to read for a minute or two, I'm sure there are pages that are just a bunch of "blah, blah, blah" to you. But while that's the case, please remember that it may be exactly what someone else needs that day, at that moment. I feel so honoured that you have let me share my heart and mind. In this life, some days are a party, and others not so much. Life is a mixed bag full of surprises—some good, some not. Even Forest Gump would agree!

Today I'd like you to think seriously about sharing your life with me. Everyone has a story. You have a story, one that is close to your heart and, therefore, close to mine. I'd love to hear from you, encourage you, and pray for you. Never underestimate your importance in the eyes of the God who made you. He loves you far beyond expression; He looks at you and sees His child, significant and prepared to fulfill His best laid plans for you (Jeremiah 29:11). He has a future for you, full of hope and driven by His promises!

Okay, so every day is not super great! The ultimate party to end all celebrations is yet to come. Today we practise. For those of you tuning in late, the title *On the Way to the Party* comes from the concept of celebrating *everything*! As I mentioned in the introduction, my dear late husband was a great believer in celebration, and I believe he got the idea from reading the Bible, the Old Testament specifically. So in our home we were always encouraged to celebrate, even what often would be considered mundane achievements. Nothing eradicates the mundane like a special dinner, a trip out for ice cream, or even something as silly as eating a meal from the "special plate," or dancing around the living room and singing!

I invite you to join in the celebration. Let me know what you're doing to create joy and excitement in your life.

Let's continue to party on the way to *the* party!

On the Way to the Party
AN ATTITUDE OF GRATITUDE

Yes, I know, that's about as cliché as you can get! But somewhere in the world, someone is celebrating Thanksgiving Day today. It got me thinking. As you may know, it doesn't take much to get me thinking, but keeping my thoughts on track … well, that's another matter altogether! I'd like to group my reflections into several categories: faith, family, fitness, finances, and fun.

First of all, I'm so grateful for the opportunity to live in a country where, so far, we have the freedom to express and practise our faith. We may feel it slipping somewhat these days, but that simply means we need to take up the challenge, stand up, and speak up for that faith. My faith consists of more than visiting a church occasionally, or watching my favourite preacher on television. It literally brings meaning and purpose to my life and, through my relationship with Jesus Christ, gives me power to live in victory over all that is harsh and cruel in this world. Thank you, God!

Next, I am forever grateful for my family: my parents, who brought me up in the faith I now cherish; my siblings, many of whom I love to emulate and others who taught me much about how *not* to live; and my children, whom I love and hold ever closer to my heart as I gain in years. And, of course, they have blessed me richly with beautiful grandchildren, my crowning glory. Clearly, when I mention my children and grandchildren, I include those I inherited with my second marriage. They have enriched my life that much more and introduced me to a new facet of family. I am so thankful for my late husband, who fulfilled my life and brought a whole set of siblings with him that I still hold dear. Now I give thanks for my husband, who blesses me every day in a way only he can, not to mention that he brought into my life a whack of new siblings, whom I appreciate more as I get to know them better. Thank you, God!

Although I won't describe myself as particularly fit, I will say that I do enjoy good health for the most part. What I'm really thankful for is the country we live in, which provides a health care system that makes it possible to get medical help. Were it not for this huge blessing, how many of us would enjoy what we have in the way of health? Thank you, God, for good health!

That thought ties in somewhat with finances. Besides being blessed with employment opportunities, the financial help afforded by our government, such as job pensions and medical assistance, makes life much easier for those who need a hand up at times. Thank you, God, for your abundant provision!

Because we are blessed to live in this country, with a buffet of various and beautiful scenic viewing opportunities to enjoy, fun and adventure are constantly at our fingertips. Again, I am thankful for the means to be able to do some travelling and see parts of this gorgeous nation of ours. Not only that, but I've travelled to different parts of the world as well. When I think that many have grown up in one city and never set foot outside its parameters, I'm even more grateful for the blessings I've experienced. Thank you, God!

With all that, I look forward to seeing the sights on "the other side." Until then, I will always remember to thank my God as I continue on the way to the party!

On the Way to the Party
PLASTIC, HIGHLY OVER-RATED

There we were, riding along in the car, anxious to get home one Sunday after church. The "animals" were getting restless, and it was feeding time at the "zoo!" I'm not sure how we got on the topic, but it turned out my little girl was missing her teddy bear and expressed how she couldn't wait to cuddle him. I half-turned in my seat and said encouragingly, "I'd be happy to cuddle you." Her response? "But Mommy, you're not cozy. You're just plastic!"

After having a little chuckle, I couldn't help but think how true it was at times. I understood then as I do now that in her four-year-old mind, my skin, although not really plastic, was smoother than a fuzzy stuffy. Her dolls were plastic, and as much as she loved them, there were times when only a cozy teddy would do!

How often I have felt myself cringe after some interaction with a friend or family member? How I must have come across as cold and heartless, showing the emotion of a plastic doll.

Jesus challenges us in His sermon on the mount to be salt and light in this world. God's Word reminds us several times to love others as we love ourselves. I guess that's the rub: all too often we don't really love ourselves as we should. We call that conceit and arrogance, yet we're not capable of truly loving another until we can love ourselves properly. It's actually insecurity and low self esteem that shows up as arrogance as we desperately try to hide who we are deep down inside.

In meeting my Lord, Jesus Christ, and building a personal relationship with Him, I am learning how my creator God feels about me, how He sees me and my friends. That makes all the difference! I'm developing a healthy love for myself, knowing that I am nothing without my Lord, but everything because of Him! Being made in the image of God Himself, I now can see others as He does; they too are made in His image. Out of a full heart I'm able to reach out and love, because I am no longer "plastic" with a heart of stone. According to Ezekiel 36:26, God promises to give us a new spirit when we turn to Him, and a soft heart of flesh in place of a heart of stone. How I thank Him for breathing this new life into me and making me usable for His purposes!

Come, walk this path with me, and let's be those flesh and blood people that actually make a difference on the way to the party!

On the Way to the Party
IT'S THE MOST WONDERFUL TIME OF THE YEAR

I'll just say it: I LOVE CHRISTMAS!

Before you go all PC on me... yes, I mean "Christmas." Not the holidays, or the season, not even family time. All of those things are special to me, but they wouldn't be if all those years ago, God hadn't taken compassion on His people and seen the need to send his son, the Christ, the anointed one. *That* is what I celebrate every year at this time.

There was a time a few years back when I loved planning and preparing my children's birthday parties. This involved theme planning, decorating, menu planning, and, of course, the cake, which I loved to bake and decorate myself! Then there was shopping for just the right gift. I loved every step, from plan to execution. I guess that's where the turn-around came—clean up not being that much fun!

If I can have that much fun with my child's birthday celebration, why not when celebrating the birth of my Lord and Saviour? When Christmas celebration planning becomes too overwhelming or unenjoyable, I have to ask myself if I'm doing everything just to impress others. Am I focusing on the why? Am I expecting more of myself than is reasonable and doable financially and physically? If that's the case, I need to step back, slow down, and do some serious readjusting of priorities.

Now with my focus in the right place, my heart full of love for my God, family, and friends, I can accomplish so much more without feeling the pressure to do so, and above all, I can enjoy it! I do love the decorating, not just the tree, but here and there throughout the house. At the end of a long day, I sit in the warm glow of the fireplace, the lights on the tree and various garlands adding to the beauty of the evening. Christmas carols playing quietly in the background add to the festive atmosphere. I can imagine with joy the excitement of the grandkids opening their gifts, and I have peace of mind knowing that the stuff is all paid for. Indeed, it is only "stuff," and I won't be receiving a bill for it next month.

I have baked a few things and plan to do a bit more, but if it doesn't happen, I'll still enjoy my Christmas and my family time to the full! It all sounds rather old fashioned, doesn't it? But that's okay, because I'm not trying to impress anyone … not even you.

I realize there are so many who are not blessed with all these trappings, but the point I'm trying to make is that the trappings and trimmings are nice, but without them I still have the reason for it all hidden deep in my heart. It's my relationship with the One whom we celebrate, the One who gives me a purpose for living every day. If I had nothing else but Him, I would have a beautiful, blessed Christmas! And that, my friend, is what I wish for you.

Come with me, and let's party on the way to the party!

On the Way to the Party
CAN YOU PAY THE PRICE?

No, I will not be giving a lecture on staying within your budget whilst Christmas shopping!

The past couple of weeks have brought my mind back to a time about eight years ago. This happens every year, causing me to reflect on such a painful time in my life that I really don't want to go there. Yet I do. On a positive note, the quick look back affords me the opportunity to be thankful for where God has brought me from, as well as reminds me that I do not have to repeat history. A quick look back being the key here. Any more, and I could totally mess up where I'm going!

Eight years ago, I called the ambulance for the last time to transport my very ill husband to the hospital. He spent the next twenty-four hours or so in a comatose condition. He then rallied and remained in hospital (other than forty-eight hours at home on a pass over Christmas) until he graduated into the presence of Jesus, his Lord, one month later.

With these memories come all the thoughts of what I shoulda, coulda, woulda done differently had I known how fleeting life is. Oh, I always knew how fragile life is, how it could change in the blink of an eye, for myself or a loved one. But you can never really *know* until you walk that path.

I remember a day just before he was told the cancer was back for the third time, and that it was angry and aggressive. He was leaving for work, and something (very small and inconsequential) happened. I made a thoughtless remark, not meaning any hurt, but realized later how it had made him feel demeaned. In the moment, his response was not nice or uplifting either. Then he left the house, and I went to empty the dishwasher, still fuming. My emotional state made it easy for a small plate to slip from my grasp and smash on the countertop. I stopped what I was doing, looked at it, and thought, *That felt GOOD! Yeah!* Then I proceeded to smash the next three on purpose, every crash feeling better than the one before!

Unfortunately, the good feeling was fleeting as I realized that a very nice set of dishes was now minus four side plates! I reached for the phone and made a very important call, after which all was clean, new, and forgiven. At that point, I realized I wasn't willing to pay the price for that kind of anger; it just wasn't worth it!

Life is too short. Those were only dishes, but there have been other times, other situations, where more was at stake. My friends, it's not worth it. Nine months later as that dear man lay in a hospital room and we were saying goodbye to each other with breaking hearts, I couldn't help but think of that morning and wish with all my heart it hadn't happened! I no longer have those dishes. (I eventually gave them away; I did not smash them all.) But as long as I had them and kept coming up short on the small plates, I would think, *What a price to pay for a small situation like that.* That tiny memory kept me from saying and doing a lot of things I would have later regretted.

As I continue down this road called *life*, my prayer for you is that you will navigate this road with only fleeting glances in the rear view mirror—just long enough to remember and learn from the past, but keep your eyes glued to what's ahead. God has great things up there for you! Keep in mind that there's a price attached to every choice you make. Forgiveness is free, but guilt will bankrupt you. Don't wallow in it.

Enjoy the ride on the way to the party!

On the Way to the Party
ONCE UPON A CHRISTMASTIME

Everyone has their own unique Christmas memory box tucked away somewhere in the back of their minds. Some of the memories are happy, some sad, others downright painful and better left alone. Yet there they are, and every once in a while they pop out and make us smile. Or laugh. Or cry.

May I share with you one of my most memorable Christmases? I was only seven, so that was almost sixty years ago. Of course, as a child, such a Christmas would revolve around the gifts received!

It was a few weeks before the Big Day, and I had been given the opportunity to see *and hold* the latest doll on the market! It was a life-size baby doll, and as a little girl I did love dolls. From that moment it was all I talked about, all I wanted to find Christmas morning! I knew chances were slim because of the astronomical cost (I believe the price was $3.98), but a kid can dream, right?

One day after school, just a few days before Christmas, I was doing my home chores, which happened to include carrying in wood from the woodpile outside. It would then be placed in a cradle-shaped box behind the cook stove in the kitchen. As I was lowering my armful of wood into the box, I realized the box was missing. I said something to this effect to

Mom, and she replied, "I needed the wood box for something else, so just put it on the floor."

Christmas Eve finally arrived, and after our church service, we went home and put our bowls and boxes on the dining table, each one at his own place. Since my oldest sister was already married and had a few children, she had come to our house with the little ones to spend the night. My brother-in -law would join us in the morning after farm chores were completed.

Don't ask me where we all slept that night! I vaguely remember being laid out across the bed with my niece and nephews. How resourceful, and plenty of room for four small kids! I guess we eventually fell asleep, because before you could say "Saint Nick," we were headed downstairs to check our loot!

There before my eyes was the one and only thing I *really* wanted: a life-size baby doll, all beautifully dressed in a dress and sweater/ bootie/ hat set that I knew instantly my mom had sewn! She was sleeping under a lovely hand-made blanket (that I still have), with her head resting on a tiny, baby-size pillow. The cradle? A new and improved, re-purposed wood box, with a fresh coat of paint and lined with wallpaper.

I was beyond excited and *so* very thankful! Then my older sister, already a teen, showed me what she had made for me: a play kitchen cupboard, manufactured out of cardboard boxes and painted white. On the counter stood the cutest little canister set made of different sized containers and decorated to look the same! Talk about recycling and re-purposing. There was no child ever more excited, and no Tiny Chef Kitchen that could hold a candle to the one made with such love and sacrifice.

The gift from my oldest sister was a beautiful dress that she had sewn, and a real, honest- to-goodness, heart-shaped locket that opened up to reveal space for a tiny picture! Again, I was over the moon, and we played house the entire day. I sometimes wonder if that was the big influence in my life. You see, all I ever wanted to do as a grown-up was to be a wife, mother, and homemaker. I've been blessed to be able to do that and fulfill my God-given desires.

For many years I had the joy of caring for real babies, the cuddly kind, and spending hours a day in a large-as-life kitchen, loving the creative process of feeding people and pouring love into their lives!

I wonder if that's how God feels about His sacrificial gift of love on that very first Christmas. Yes, love and sacrifice are what Christmas is really all about. As an adult, I understand this, but I believe the foundation was laid in seeing it acted out before the eyes of an impressionable child.

Let's keep it real this Christmas and let the love of God flow all around us as we head toward the party!

On the Way to the Party
MOVING ON …

I'm a great believer in using the rear view mirror. I know you can't drive using only that; it's also important to use the windshield and keep your eyes on the road ahead. However, it's a good idea to occasionally glance back and see what's catching up with you, checking to make sure you're leaving the past behind and thereby ensuring that you're moving in a forward direction.

Translate that into life: Every morning is the gift of a new day! Every new day brings fresh opportunities, unused potential, and new insights. Because of where you've already been, you've learned a few things that hopefully enable you to make choices and decisions that are less likely to end in disaster.

When looking back on the past year and life in general, I'm amazed at all the blessings that have been showered on me! I refuse to blandly pass over them and take them for granted. I've lived long enough to know that life can easily go off the rails, and you end up nowhere near where you want to be. I also have seen the hand of Mighty God work in my life situations and change disappointment to delight! My Bible tells me in John 10 that the enemy comes to kill, steal, and destroy, but Jesus came to give me abundant (overflowing) life! I'll take the latter. Jeremiah

29:11 also states that God knows the plans He has for me. I will take this with me into the year ahead!

The year behind held its heartaches and challenges, which I choose not to dwell on. It also brought a lot of blessings, some of which I'd like to share with you. In October of 2017, I was finally able to have corrective surgery on my right foot after a twenty-eight-year-old injury. Since then, my body has begun to straighten out, and pain is almost non-existent. I thank God for this and especially for allowing me to be born and grow up in this country where such medical care is available. As I've already written, God granted me a wonderful miracle in the straightening of my toes without surgery!

Then there was the wonderful time I spent re-connecting with family at a reunion in July. Some of those dear people I hadn't seen for almost twenty years!

I was also blessed this past summer to do some walking activities that were impossible to take part in for years. More to come!

I've been privileged to be involved in an outreach program for people living in challenging situations. I've loved it, and I'm excited to continue in the new year!

Through my church, I've also become involved in a small group that encourages building relationships through creating a great balance between Bible study, serving opportunities, and fun times. I can't wait to see what awaits me in the year ahead!

I do know that whatever is yet to come, with my Lord and Shepherd walking alongside me, I will again experience many blessings and challenges.

In the meantime, I continue on and invite you to join me on the way to the party!

On the Way to the Party
YOU A IDIOT 'DO?

Okay, I admit, that's a weird title. But wait! I can explain. Years ago, when my oldest grandson was visiting for the day, we had the sweetest conversation. I still think about it, and it has become my daily challenge.

He was all of two years old and happily playing and chattering all day. At one point I went to pull out the vacuum cleaner and get something done. I turned it on, and the dust began to fly. I checked and found that the bag had been removed but not replaced with a new one. As happens occasionally, my mouth went into gear and I said something like, "Some idiot didn't replace the bag!" I thought I was talking to myself but quickly realized I had a little audience when a tiny voice questioned, "You a idiot, Gwamma?" I tried talking my way out of that one by assuring him I wasn't but was sure someone else was. He simply cocked his head to one side and, looking very puzzled, repeated, "Gwamma, you a idiot 'do?"

Well, I'm still not sure, maybe you know, but like I said before, I often think of that. It has made me more determined than ever to cease and desist from laying that or any other label on others. More than that, I've been trying very hard not to act like one myself. Some days I think I am successful!

Since a new year has just begun, I've been making an extra effort to make my life count for good and for God. I don't do New Year's resolutions. Been there, done that, don't have the t-shirt or anything to show for it. I do like to plan my direction for the next year, praying for God's leading and then holding my plans and accompanying goals in an open hand. One thought that's been pressing on my mind lately is this: "It is never too late, and I am never too old!" I was well into my fifties when I decided to take some art classes, because I've always wanted to express myself in the beauty of painting. I was past sixty when I published my first book. As a child, I badly wanted to take piano lessons, and it never happened for me. It only hit me recently that there's nothing stopping me now, so guess what … I am now the owner of a new keyboard, and so far, I'm just playing around on it when my husband's not present to hear my joyful noise! I have committed to seeking out and taking real lessons in the near future. And now that it's out there, I've made myself accountable. And it feels *good*! There is still so much life to live and so much to live for. Gone are the idiot days. Gwamma's on the go, so fasten your seatbelt!

God has awesome plans for my life and yours according to Jeremiah 29:11. I know I refer to this verse often, and that's because I have found so much inspiration in it. I want to get to the finish line and know that I've made every effort to fulfill my God-given potential. And on that note, I will leave you and continue on the way to the party!

On the Way to the Party
STOP YOUR COMPLAINING!

So you'll never guess what I'm hearing these days! "It's so cold out there!" "I'm freezing!" "I can't believe how cold it is." Yes, we've heard it all. For the past few months, we've had beautiful weather, but if the temperatures hung around ten degrees for a day or two and then suddenly dipped all the way down to four, the complaints were readily hauled out! And folks, I'm talking about December and January! Now we are actually experiencing seasonal temperatures. Just wait, in three months we'll be putting up with "Oh it's sooo hot!" And that's my rant for today.

It has simply become a bad habit to complain about most everything. We live in a beautiful part of the world. And no, it's not too cold in the winter or too hot in the summer. The government, although not perfect, is better than in many other parts of the world. We have medical care, even if it doesn't always work the way we'd like. Paved highways, warm vehicles and houses in the winter months, and air conditioning in the summer all bring a boost to our quality of living.

We are so blessed, and though there are many variations of life-quality, with many of us having more opportunities and material wealth, overall this is not a Third World country, and we have so much to be thankful for.

Philippians 2:14–16 comes to mind. These verses speak against murmuring and complaining. The whole point of living is to shine in our generation, and in the end be assured that we did not run the race nor do the work in vain!

How awesome is that! Our creator knew that our natural bent would be negative, and He desires to shape and mould us into people that positively "shine" with His glory! So for the remainder of winter, and in spring when the rain comes (too much for some and not enough for others), when the heat of summer rolls in waves over us, and the funnel clouds threaten to destroy us, remember that for every negative there *has* to be a positive. It really all comes down to choice: Is the glass half empty or half full?

I've made my choice. I am here, and I have to travel this road called life. I can do it grumbling and complaining, or I can do it with a smile on my face and know in the end that I didn't live in vain!

And so I continue cheerfully on the way to the party!

On the Way to the Party
SO LOVE, EH?

So today is the day all eyes and ears are turned to LOVE! Actually, by the time you read this, the day will be in the past and, for many, no more thought will be given to this very broad subject until next year at this time.

I think of the love exchanged between friends, of which I am blessed to have many. It's easy-going and casual, not too many demands, and if it becomes uncomfortable, there's an easy escape hatch. People grow apart and life takes us down different roads, quite often into the path of new friendships. Many friendships change so much they become a bit like a cocoon, distant and dormant for a time, then emerging to prove themselves more steadfast and beautiful than you can imagine!

As a teenager, I had a special friend in high school. I'm ashamed to admit that I allowed the friendship to lapse. We both got married, had babies, raised them, and got old(er)! Several years ago, I found some contact information for her. No awkward moments … it was like not a stitch in time had passed. It's different, though. Now we enjoy a more mature relationship, both having gone through some difficult times and bearing the scars, both having come through stronger and more beautiful of spirit. Yes, sort of like a butterfly busting out of the confines of immaturity and embracing who it has become, bringing life and beauty to its corner of the world!

Then there is family! Nine years ago, our children all decided to converge on our house for Family Day weekend. February 14 happened to fall on a Sunday that year; on Saturday, we all went to Banff and spent a lovely day doing various activities together. The next day was party time with birthday celebrations, cake and all, since my birthday just happens to fall on Valentine's Day. What a fun time that was, and even more special because it was the last time we enjoyed family time with all of us there and healthy. Less than three months later, we were told that cancer had metastasized in their dad's body and moved into his bones. Less than a year later, he had left this earth for his heavenly home. That weekend will always stand in my memory as a time to treasure!

Then there is the love between sweethearts. This can be anywhere from nineteen to ninety and beyond. Love has no boundaries, age or otherwise. In fact, the further it spreads, the richer it becomes, and the richer the life it pours out of! Seems ironic, doesn't it? The more love you pour out, the more you have yourself. This is especially true in romantic love; the more you share of yourself, the more fulfilled you'll be. Hold back and life seems empty.

Yes, love has many faces. Just this morning I was informed that my honorary niece had given birth to a baby girl, on my birthday no less! I was beyond ecstatic and just a little bit in love! And I haven't met this child yet!

The best and greatest love of course is the love God has shown for us. My Bible says that while we were sinners, He sent His only son to live and die for us so that we could have a relationship with the creator God. In that unlovable state, He loved us first so that we can have the ability to love Him back. I can't think of a greater love than that, can you?

So now being confident in the love of Jesus, my spouse and family and friends, I will walk in love toward others on the way to the party!

On the Way to the Party
JUST TRUST

In less than five days, we'll be far away, south of here, trudging through sand dunes, having left the snow drifts far behind! It can't come a day too soon for me as I eagerly look forward to soaking up some warmth into these old bones.

Upon hearing of our impending trip to Mexico, many people have shared cautionary words, and I do appreciate the concern. The news reports coming from the area we intend to visit aren't so encouraging either … almost to the point where we want to re-think our plans. But wait! We stop and engage a little common sense, and in so doing we realize that if we stick to the safe zone, in this case our resort and legitimate excursion tour groups, we'll be relatively safe. We don't plan to set foot on the outside on our own or do any individual adventuring. Having done all we know to do to protect ourselves, which, by the way, God expects of us anyway, we trust Him for His overall protection.

Isn't this the way every day should play out, after all? Instead of charging ahead without giving thought to the safety factors and moral quality of our plans, should we not take the time to think things through and weigh the pros and cons of our potential decision? After coming to the conclusion we feel is best and that God has led us to, we can proceed with confidence and trust Him for the outcome. I've tried to live by this principle most of my life, and I've never been let down. At times things shouldn't have worked in my favour, humanly speaking, but I serve a God who operates above all human logic and reasoning!

So as the day draws near, I will pack cheerfully, not fearfully, with a smile as bright as the sunshine I anticipate. I will rise at three in the morning and fly away. And I will trust. Trust that God will get us there safely, keep us there safely, and bring us home again in safety! More than that, I will trust that as we're enjoying our little break, God will cross our paths with someone who needs His touch and allow them to soak up His love, even as we are soaking up the sun. It's the way I prefer to live my days here at home, and nothing will be different there, except that I wouldn't dream of burying my bare toes in a snow bank! I just trust that God will use me where He needs me the most.

So it makes no difference to me what country I happen to be in. I want to bring a smile to a face here or there as I make my way to the party!

On the Way to the Party
SAND OR SNOW? HOT OR COLD?

Now that's the million dollar question this time of year when all of us living in the north of the Northern Hemisphere are getting winter weary. Longing for a pleasant change in the weather, we decided that we'd have to be the engineers of change for ourselves. We went, we saw, we enjoyed, and now we're back! We are back and we are brown, or rather, in my case, a little bit red.

One thing that always amazes me is that no matter the country of origin, the culture, or the race, people are all the same on the inside. One of the reasons I love travelling is to meet other races and get to know a little bit about their cultures. I see many more similarities than differences. We all get happy, excited, and sad about the same things. Some people are kind and compassionate no matter where they happen to live, while others are impatient and miserable in the same circumstances.

I was reminded again recently that there is no one race or culture that has the corner on cheating and deceitfulness; these attributes just seem to attach themselves to anyone who welcomes them!

Right here and now I'd like to give honour to the beautiful people of Mexico I had the privilege of meeting last week. As a tourist using a cane for stability support, I wasn't the fastest car on the track, yet I encountered only kindness and caring wherever I went. To all those wonderful guides, drivers, and waiters (you know who you are), I say "Thank you" from the bottom of my heart. You made our time in your country so much more pleasant than it might have been!

On the last day of our stay I enjoyed a cool dip in the ocean, dunking myself several times only to discover in horror as I returned to the sandy beach that I had forgotten to remove my waist pack before going into the water! In it were my cell phone, passport, and Mexican immigration certificate, which I needed to present in order to leave the country.

The phone ended up in the cell phone "hospital," where we hoped it could be repaired and recovered! The passport was fine after a session with the blow dryer. The certificate was dried after the same fashion but came out looking worse for wear. At the airport, it was not accepted until it received a special stamp at the immigration office. We were able to locate the office, get the stamp, and still make it to our boarding gate on time, not knowing that our flight would be delayed two hours.

While we waited there, the young man from the check-in counter came through. He recognized me and stopped to asked if I'd been able to find the immigration office and get my stamp. I assured him all was well and accomplished and then thanked him for his concern. He seemed genuinely pleased that he was able to help me.

That's what I mean, folks. Most people enjoy being helpful and going the extra mile! As a follower of Jesus Christ, I believe that's how He wants me to live. He made it clear as He walked and talked with His disciples on this earth, teaching them that if anyone asked them for their sweater (my version), they were to give him their coat as well. Or if someone asked them to walk a mile with him, they should walk two miles. Yes, the ungodly are the same the world over, and those who belong to the Lord God are also the same, no matter where they live.

I'm determined that wherever I am, and whatever road I travel, I will be one willing to walk that extra mile or kilometre. After all, I'll only get there faster, and *I am* on my way to the party!

On the Way to the Party
IN ALL HONESTY

Not that I'm ever dishonest with you … I just try to take a more positive position. I have found that negativity only drags others down a level or two, and at the same time pulls me even lower. Having said that, I confess that tonight I come with a heart full of sadness. A friend and neighbour stopped in this evening with her little dog. I met her only last summer, and Zorro was her faithful companion—always there, always ready for a little bit of lovin'. He was up there in doggie years but had a lot of love and adoration to give in return for a pat on the head. A couple of months ago, she became aware that he wasn't well. Now, after a long time on medications with no improvement but rather continuing weight loss, she had to make a decision. She carried him to my house and in tears announced that he was going to "doggie heaven" tomorrow morning. My heart aches for a friend who is losing a much loved, faithful companion of fourteen plus years!

I'll even miss the little fur ball; he loved to curl up at our feet under my kitchen table as we chatted over coffee or lunch. I could see the decline in health and weight as his spine and ribs became more pronounced. Yes, he's not human, but he is one of God's creations, and it makes me sad to think of the grief my friend will endure. My family also lost a long-time furry friend when our children were younger, and it hurts.

The first few weeks of coming home from somewhere and not being greeted at the door with doggy kisses drove us all to our bedroom, where we hugged and cried for a while. Eventually, these occurrences happened less and less often, as grief was washed out a little more each time. No, she will never forget him, but the sharpness of the pain of missing him will become less. As we know, the God of all comfort comforts us in all our sorrows, whether the loss of a human companion or other.

The awesome thing about my God is that He meets me wherever I am; He wants to meet you wherever you are. He's not limited to certain situations. There are way too many things that can cause heartache in life, and God is aware of His hurting children. I pray that we all will become more aware of Him and His propensity to bring healing and wholeness to the ones He loves.

That's my heart tonight as I continue on the way to the party.

On the Way to the Party
HEY! WHAT HAPPENED?

We weren't planning to take a warm climate vacation this year, but when someone puts a thought in your mind, sometimes you can't get rid of it. No matter how often you pop yourself upside the head and yell, "Get out, get out, get out!" it just won't leave. So what do you do? I'll tell you what to do. You go online, find the warmest place that appeals to you, book it for the earliest possible date, pull out your credit card, and pack your bag. It's quite simple, really!

Here we are now, home for two weeks, and spring has actually sprung! When we arrived back from the south it was still extremely cold. Then the time change happened and, soon after, the first day of spring. During this speedy transition, my energy was still lagging somewhat, and then suddenly this burst hit me and I ended up planning so much into my days, I found it hard to find time for all the exciting things, like laundry and vacuuming!

Oh, so you can relate?

I just want to say that I love this time of year! There are so many opportunities to pick up the pace and spruce things up in and around the house. Not only that, but these are things I never even thought of doing, or noticed needed doing, six weeks ago. Now everything is kicked into high gear, and I love the energy I get from the planning. And there's always enough time to get the job done.

Then there's the issue of hibernation, which happens to us all in varying degrees every winter. The older I get, the more comfortable that becomes! Last month, the most likely thing for me to do after supper was sit in my recliner with my feet up while reading a good book, watching TV, or working on a word search! Tonight, I suddenly got the urge to go for a drive and pick up ice cream. How I hate it when those urges hit me! But it did, and we did. A beautiful sunset later, we arrived back home, and I sighed and thanked God that spring has actually arrived. Oh yes, more snow is coming, but it won't be more than a tiny, cat-like sneeze in the grand scheme of things!

In Genesis 8, we read of the great biblical flood and its aftermath. When Noah and his family exited the ark and made a thanksgiving sacrifice to God, He was pleased and promised mankind that as long as the earth remains, we will consistently see seed time and harvest, cold and heat, winter and summer, as well as day and night. All those thousands of years ago, and it still stands! God has not changed the order of things. I believe I am safe in putting my life in His hands and trusting Him to keep all the other promises He has made to His children!

Summer or winter, I choose to trust Him as I continue on the way to the party!

On the Way to the Party
RISING ABOVE

It seems everywhere I turn lately, I'm staring this challenge in the face! The other day I was reading an article that spoke about people who live their entire lives looking up at the bottom of life, and what could have been if they had only been given a few breaks along the way. Then I watched a talk show on television that spoke to the same issue, bringing up the fact that many blame their parents and/or siblings for all the hardships they've endured. This not only causes the pain of resentment and unforgiveness to become a burden they seem destined to carry, but it also makes it difficult for other family members to reach them with love. The wall becomes so high and reinforced over the course of many years, no loving acts or encouraging words can penetrate it.

As I see it, not one human alive has always had things go their way. Everyone deals with issues and challenges, although I realize that some have suffered greatly in comparison to others. Ironically, often it's those who have come out of the darkest situations that rise above and shine much brighter than the rest of us! Then I have to say to myself, "Sister, you have nothing to complain about!"

When I hear full grown adults cast blame on something that happened years ago, a part of me just wants to scream out, "Suck it up, Princess!" I thank God that in those moments His compassion reigns, and I see the hurting child and pain-filled adult who is stuck and has no idea how to move forward.

What saddens me more than anything else is to hear our beloved seniors in their seventies, eighties, and beyond express bitterness and resentment as they recount stories of their childhood six or seven decades ago. To them I want to say, "Go back there!" Let your emotions carry you back and think of all the ones that should have loved and protected you. It's too late to receive anything from them, so crawl into the lap of your *loving* Father God. Allow Him to wrap His arms of love around you and hug you tight. Let His compassion and acceptance seep into your very soul and ooze into every crevice of your scab-hardened heart. Let forgiveness flow for those that have hurt you; in doing so, you free yourself from their continued control. As the heaviness begins to lift, you will find yourself rising like a hot air balloon, with all resistance gone. Don't think it can happen? I *know* it can. I am one living example, and I know of many more!

I would be happy to introduce you to others, if you'll come and walk with me on the way to the party!

On the Way to the Party
OOPS! I BLEW IT!

A s a child, I made a promise. There have been times in my pretty long life that I've kept it, and too many times when I haven't. I can imagine you thinking, *Well, you were only a child. Children don't always know what they're doing or saying.* But this promise wasn't empty or made thoughtlessly. I knew even at a young age that the hand of God was on me, and He had a special plan and purpose for my life. Therefore, when I made a promise to Him that I would serve Him happily, I meant it!

Isn't it strange how promises can roll off the tongue so easily yet be so hard to keep? There's a price to be paid when we're compelled to deliver. It isn't always convenient to follow that tug of God on my heart; sometimes it takes a little bit of time, or a little bit of cash! I wish I could say that I only blew it when I was a young, thoughtless kid, but often it happened as an adult, knowing full well what I was doing, how I was grieving the heart of the One who loves me more than anyone else could, and being fully aware of the blessings missed in the process.

I know I can't do enough good to save the world, or even to make a dent in all that needs doing. This I do know—when I obey God, it makes a difference for *someone*! It makes a dent in one person's life. That makes all the difference to me. I've learned, and am still learning, that God never intended for me to be the answer to everyone's prayer; I simply need to be obedient in what God asks of me! There's always someone on the other side of my obedience, and it's not good enough for me to depend on others to fulfill my call to a task.

So yes, I have blown it many times, and I'm sure I will again. I know that every time I blow it, my heart breaks for my carelessness, and I come away with renewed commitment to serve where I can. This is what fulfills me; this is what gives me purpose.

I wish that everyone out there finds the peace and experiences the joy I've found in keeping a promise I made to my God as a young child. As I continue down this path called life, I pray that the eyes and ears of my heart will always be open to see opportunities as they come up. This should keep me busy on the way to the party!

On the Way to the Party
TRANSFORMATION

I wonder how many people actually like doing housework. It's more likely that we do the necessary work simply because it needs to be done, and someone has to do it! I've heard people say that they enjoy cleaning, and I wouldn't dare argue the point. However, I do understand where they are coming from, I think.

Recently, I had opportunity to do a little more cleaning than usual, and I can get a little high on it! Just today when I was cleaning bathrooms and mopping floors, I thought to myself, *Do I really enjoy this, as I've declared more than once, or is it the finished product that motivates me?* After giving it a little thought, it occurred to me that I'm most fascinated by the transforming process! I walk into a room that obviously needs some work, and then I begin the task, no matter how unpleasant, and in a short time I see a marked difference as the beauty sparkles through! The room is transformed!

It brings to mind the redeeming work of God in the life of a person given over to Him. No matter how messed up, tangled, or confused one is, the power of Jesus Christ and the blood He shed to redeem us back to God comes in and begins a transforming work. That life will never be perfected on this side of eternity, but as the Holy Spirit is given space and permission to freely work, a lasting transformation takes place. The result that follows will sparkle with the love and life of our Lord!

I've seen with my own eyes how one with a seriously scary addiction to illicit drugs has given his life to Christ and currently exudes the sparkle of love and joy that comes only from Jesus. I've seen couples whose relationships were twisted to the point of breaking until God heard them in their heartache and despair, stepped in, and did a bit of housecleaning. The transformation is like no other, possibly because He has the power to do so much more than a fix. He makes us brand new: *"… anyone who belongs to Christ has become a new person. The old life has gone; a new life has begun!"* (2 Corinthians 5:17, NLT).

True transformation can only be complete when we realize our authority and freedom in Christ: *"There is therefore now no condemnation to them which are in Christ Jesus, who do not walk according to the flesh, but according to the Spirit."* (Romans 8:1). We can know that we belong to Jesus and are included in the family of God as we relate to Him as a child to a loving Father. Then take a peek inside and see how He is changing attitudes, outlook, and habits; these small changes are proof of a solid transformation that will bring BIG results!

Come join me on the way to the party!

On the Way to the Party
HIS HEART FOR YOU

Some time ago, I wrote the section entitled "God Doesn't Care." He doesn't care in that He loves us through everything we've ever done, no matter how horrible, careless, or wasteful. God loves us right where we are, and He loves us too much to leave us like that. Today I'd like to present to you a God who cares far beyond where our finite minds can travel!

As a child, I often asked: "Why is it called Good Friday when it wasn't good at all? It was sad, and they hurt Jesus so bad, even though He never did anything wrong!" Here's what I was told and what I now believe and experience daily: It's good because it's good for us. God had so much love for us, He sent His own son to earth to live as a man, to give up His life through a cruel death on the cross so that I could come freely into God's presence and have a part in all that He has for me in this life as well as in life with Him in eternity. It sounds so simple, yet it took all of the heart of an eternal God to put that plan into action. As Jesus hung on the cross, He declared "*It is finished!*" (John 19:30). In those three little words, He packed a promise that what He was doing meant we would never have to pay the price required to have a relationship with our creator God; the cost was taken care of in a fashion that was both cruel and complete.

After the cross came the burial and then the resurrection! The work is completed. Jesus ascended to the Father and is now preparing a place for all who have accepted His finished work on the cross.

My heart is too full to express it all. I thank my God every day for the freedom and victory I experience simply by believing. I cannot help but desire to serve Him in every way I can. It seems to me there are so many needs, yet I certainly don't feel guilt over being limited in meeting them all. I listen for that small voice that tells me where I should get involved, and I trust God to put other needs on the hearts of His other children. There is no condemnation, only joy, freedom, and victory in being obedient to the call on my life!

This, I believe, is a reflection of what is in the heart of Almighty God, and this is all I want others to see as I travel down this road on the way to the party!

On the Way to the Party
BOLOGNA SANDWICHES? REALLY?

While out driving from here to there today, something reminded me of an event that happened years ago. While living in a different city, my late husband and I felt led to open our home to assist people who were leaving a local cult. Our help consisted of snatching them from the tight reign of their community, as well as having them stay in our home until family were notified or they were able to get established with jobs and/or permanent living arrangements.

One young gentleman brought a smile to my face more than once; he was a gentle soul, always offering to help with one project or another. "Frank" (as I will call him) especially enjoyed helping me with the grocery shopping. With four growing children of our own, plus several that were enrolled in our home daycare, along with the extras that lived with us ... well, grocery shopping was a major weekly excursion!

Frank convinced me to buy several hundred grams of bologna at the local deli. As he proceeded to explain how much he loved bologna sandwiches and had been deprived of this treat the entire time he was ensconced in the cult, I could almost imagine him drooling. Of course, once we got the groceries put away at home, I offered him a sandwich. He smiled broadly as he set about building it. Not one, two, or even three slices of the slimy red stuff went into this masterpiece—it took five slices to complete the task, after which he wolfed it down and sat back with a huge grin of satisfaction!

Frank stayed with us for three weeks before his parents came to retrieve him and take him home to eastern Canada. During this time, we celebrated my husband's birthday. I made a large cake and bought a barrel of ice cream. We invited a few friends to join us for an impromptu party. Again, Frank impressed us with the lack they had endured while in the cult. He enjoyed two ginormous servings of cake and ice cream before declaring himself full. Frank was a young man with a rather petite build! He and the other two people we were harbouring all claimed to have not tasted these goodies in six years!

I didn't see bologna sandwiches as a big treat, so I was just a bit amused by the whole thing. Yet my heart went out to people who had lived in such depravity that this was something to look forward to and celebrate!

I can't help but wonder how many of God's children are extremely satisfied with the cheapest quality of life. Our heavenly Father desires to provide a lovely steak dinner for His kids, yet we desire only bologna sandwiches! Jesus states in John 10:10b: "*I have come that they may have live, and that they may have it more abundantly.*" Imagine for a moment what "more abundantly" would look like in your life. Whether in the arena of relationships, finances, business, or our faith walk, God wants to get involved and give us the best! Sometimes the best comes with a price tag we're not willing to pay. Let me assure you that it's worth paying the price and receiving the abundance God offers us in Jesus Christ!

As for me, I am done with the bologna of this life and am ready to feast on the good stuff on my way to the party!

On the Way to the Party
STRUGGLE THROUGH THE "PLUNKY"

I'm sure you've had days like that—everything just seems to be a struggle and requires that extra effort to push through. Then you wake up the next morning and sail through the day with hardly any effort at all.

Just the other day I was plodding through my keyboard lesson with great heaviness. In utter discouragement, I turned to my teacher and expressed my frustration at the "plunky," very unbeautiful sounds coming from said instrument! She offered her encouragement with these words: "Sometimes you have to struggle through the plunky for a while, and then suddenly you get it. It clicks and begins to sound entirely different, better!" Then it begins to be more fun than hard work.

Yes, I thought, so many things in life are like that … difficult and challenging for sure, but if you push through, those very same challenges can be turned into joy and fulfillment. Then one day you look back on all you've accomplished, and the pain of the struggle becomes a distant memory. The plunky has become a beautiful melody as it plays out the song that is your life!

Where are you in your life right now? Are you in the struggle stage? Are you beginning to see and feel the cadence of your purpose in life? The psalmist David had a lot to say about music and what it does for the soul. In fact, He demonstrated how music can calm fears and settle the anxious heart when he played his harp for the very disturbed King Saul.

Nine years ago when my first husband became very ill, I began a struggle like no other, and for the next eight months felt like I was literally plunking my way through every day. After the ultimate tearing apart in death, I felt the strength of my God in a way I'd never experienced before, and one day I realized the walk was indeed becoming easier. I found truth in the phrase "practice makes perfect." Not that I woke one day and found that I'd achieved perfection, but in doing every day what I had to do, I was becoming better at it, and the plunkiness had evolved to an easy rhythm that was much more pleasant to live with.

If you have a moment, I invite you to grab your Bible and read Psalm 81. It will calm your clamouring mind and bring rest to your tired body; the struggle will fade away as you give in to the music that God made you to be!

As for me, I will plunk my way through the struggle and serenade myself with lovely music on the way to the party!

On the Way to the Party
MEMORY LANE

Okay, so recent days have spilled their share of reminiscence into my life, and I'm still walking in a thin-mist nostalgia! On a two-day trip from our home to Winnipeg, we spent many hours following trails from my husband's past, and then adding some of my own. As we ate dinner in a small-town grill, I explained how some of my high school days culminated in trips to that very place and, if memory serves, even the very table we were at.

It's good to look back and remember: good times, sad times, hard times, times we can learn from, and even times that will simply make us feel good and bring on the warm fuzzies! It may not be a great idea to keep our eyes focused on where we've come from if we fail to pay attention to what is ahead; however, they both have their part to play.

Soon we would be heading to our final destination to spend some quality time with grandchildren! Here comes the fun part, and here is where we turn our focus to the future. We can look forward to being challenged, taught, laughed at, and of course entertained! Kids grow up so fast, it's difficult to keep up with their progress. Yet I find they're very accommodating and willing to educate us on their current "kick."

Philippians 3:13 challenges me to forget what is behind and "strain" toward the goal that is ahead. No, I will never actually forget; whatever happened in my past formed me and caused me to develop into the person I am today. But I no longer focus on my past; rather, I move on and turn my thoughts and efforts toward the future and those things that are still in the making. I observe with joy how God can take one incident and use it to teach me a much needed lesson, to encourage me or someone else, or in some cases to just plant His love on me and keep me moving ahead for one more day!

Yes, I do love the occasional meander down memory lane, but more than that, I love that I can look ahead and see clearly and unhindered the path before me, because it's the only way to walk on the way to the party!

On the Way to the Party
SINGIN' IN THE RAIN

On my all-day drive, I allowed my mind to wander, and it took me on a rather meandering path, stopping for moments at various locations, not all of them happy. In my own life I remember many deep, dark, stormy days when I truly felt there would never be an end to the intense sting of the driving rain of despair and hopelessness. I knew the promises of God, and I had no doubt that my God would deliver on them, but until …

I have just enjoyed a week with family, children, grandchildren, and siblings. During this short time, several people I know have lost loved ones, others have had terrible family and relationship challenges thrown at them, and still others have lost big time in the financial arena.

God has never promised that we would be without trials or tribulations, but He did promise to walk with us through the storm and to calm the turmoil inside of us! In John 16:33, we read: *"These things I have spoken to you, that in Me you may have peace. In the world you will have tribulation; but be of good cheer, I have overcome the world."* I'm not sure about you, but when I read that verse of scripture, I feel like I just opened the umbrella and stepped into its shelter from the driving rain! If you have the opportunity, check out the song "I Am" by Crowder. The soothing lyrics bringing to life the promises of our Lord and Saviour will wash over your soul that has been ravaged by the storms of life.

I have found Jesus to be my companion in every storm thrown at me, but only in as much as I have allowed Him access. A lot of my encouragement has come in the form of music, and I guess that's why I tend to start singing when the rain begins to fall. Actually, God often brings gentle rains into our lives, not to overwhelm us, but to refresh us and stimulate growth. These are never meant to destroy and devastate!

Tomorrow as I finish the journey home, I see that the forecast calls for rain. Although I don't particularly like driving in the rain, I plan to be singin' in it and sailing along in the peace of Jesus on my way to the party!

On the Way to the Party
LOOKING BEYOND

It's that time of year again. After the cold harshness of winter, the warmth of the sun creeps into the nooks and crannies of the yard and melts away every chilling trace of snow and ice. My fingers itching to play in the dirt, I donned my gardening gloves and went to work cleaning out last year's old growth, now dead and dry. Next came the task of preparing the soil for new planting, setting out pots that will hopefully soon contain rainbows of colour that will cheer my days, and cleaning up the little accessories that welcome my fine-feathered friends to stop over!

As my hands became busy with the chore before me, I thought about how great the yard would look when the job was done and how clean and light my soul feels when I tidy up and rid myself of mental and emotional "stuff" that builds up and tries to take over. I realize that after a good spiritual shower in the cleansing Word of God, I not only feel cleaner and better but look better and more appealing as a child of God.

I've been attending group meetings with the purpose of seeking healing and freedom from hurts, habits, and hang-ups. At this time, we're learning how to take inventory, and, frankly, I'm finding it much more difficult than I imagined, especially having walked in my faith in

Jesus Christ for many years. I'm learning that it's never too late to learn more about walking clean and free!

As my hands got busy, so did my mind, and this parallel was impressed on it: There is always negative influence in my life that needs guarding against and plucking out. There are always bad attitudes popping up that need to be discarded. Left alone, they wreak havoc in my relationships with God and the people I love. After the cleaning out process is completed, there is now room for new growth, resulting in a kaleidoscope of colour and joyful purpose. I pray that I will look like that as by the grace of God I find the courage to stay on top of the "weeds" that enter my life!

Now at the end of a tiring day, I know my work will not be in vain, as others enter my yard throughout the summer months and see what was accomplished and experience the calm, peace, and comfort as a result. I am reminded that even Jesus prayed in the garden before His arrest and crucifixion: "Please remove this task from before me; nevertheless, not my will but yours be done" (Matthew 26:39, paraphrased). He went through with the entire plan of salvation because He looked forward to restoring His children to a relationship with Him.

In Hebrews 12:2, we read that because of the *"joy that was set before Him* [He] *endured the cross, despising the shame, and has sat down at the right hand of the throne of God."* Yes, it's been a big day, and yes, I'm just a wee bit exhausted, but it feels good to know that because I persevered, good things are to come!

And this is how I roll on the way to the party!

On the Way to the Party
LIFT THEM UP!

At some point every summer it seems that a haze creeps into our city. My first thought is always, *It's overcast.* By the third day, I realize it has everything to do with the wild fires in the northern part of the province. Now the scent of smoke is causing a choking feeling to come over me, and I have no allergies or history of asthma! The intensity of the smoke is almost unbelievable considering the fires are hundreds of kilometres away.

My heart goes out to the residents in the affected communities and those fighting the seemingly endless battle there. I try to put myself in their place: seeing the glow coming closer, hearing the roar and the crackling, and knowing you have to evacuate and choose the most important things to pack and take along. Just trying to imagine makes my heart heavy.

Once you're on the road, you know you're facing ... what? You can't be sure where you and your loved ones will end up, *if* your loved ones are with you. In many cases, men opt to stay and fight, which adds a whole new stress to the scenario. Families are separated and aren't sure when they'll be reunited. Wherever you end up for the duration, you wonder if the townspeople will accept you and show compassion, or see you as an added burden to their already over-taxed community. Will they resent your presence among them?

So many things perking and turning in your tired brain. Then there's the issue of provision; not everyone has a bank account that will sustain them for several months away from home and consistent employment. Even when they're eventually allowed back, there might not be employment if it all went up in flames.

May I appeal to every kind, compassionate cell in your heart today? Do what you can in the way of assistance. If you live close enough to offer an extra hand, do it! Financial help is always welcome, and of course there is the avenue of prayer. While we may not know the people affected or involved, God does, and we can leave it in His very capable hands. If you know someone caught in the midst of this tragedy, let them know you care. Love and compassion are always in style!

In this very short life, I've found that people will always respond to a kind, caring word and a smile. Please remember to use these tools freely as you continue on your way to the party.

On the Way to the Party

RAVES AND RAMBLINGS FROM THE ROAD

Hitting the road early Tuesday morning (not as early as we wanted, though … *never* as early as we wanted), we had plans for the next five days. After dozing off for a while, we arrived at the south Alberta border crossing. The officer there put us on the spot when he asked where we were headed. The reply: "Kalispell."

In surprise he responded, "What in the world can you get in Kalispell that you can't get in Calgary?"

My husband assured him it was only our destination for the day and loosely laid out our plans further down the road. As we began to drive, we figured out that this small city across the border did indeed have quite a bit to offer us: Hobby Lobby, beautiful scenery, and last but not least, Krispy Kreme doughnuts! When I spied the doughnut store, I insisted we stop so I could pick up a few pre-dunked goodies. I ordered two but was told to return after 5:00, since that was when the baking would begin.

Later when I entered the store, the young cashier brought me a box filled with a "hole" dozen of the tasty treats! I was trying to explain that it wasn't my order when along came the manager and told me to take my box and get out! The nerve! Again in shock, I tried to explain that I'd only ordered two pastries. Again he told me to take it and leave. As a last resort, I asked for the bill so I could pay for them. He responded in a stern voice, insisting I take the box and leave "before I call security!"

At that point I noticed the smirk on his face and got the heck out of Dodge! Or Krispy Kreme, or whatever! What a blessing! We shared them with family when we arrived back in BC. I did figure out why I love them unglazed: they taste just like the ones my mom made when I was a kid! That alone was enough reason to cross the border; next time, I will have a proper answer!

Besides all that, we got a head start on our Christmas shopping, visited family, and even reunited with a sweet cousin of mine whom I hadn't seen in at least fifteen years. Today on the first leg of our journey home, we had a ferry ride and visited some artisan shops, where we viewed a broom maker at work and enjoyed perusing his wares. It was here that my husband suggested I might be interested in purchasing a new vehicle!

Further down the road, we toured a glass house made entirely of embalming fluid bottles! I know, right? I couldn't help but wonder how many lives, or rather, deaths, were represented there. Six hundred thousand bottles later, and the owner had his retirement home!

And on that note, I am about ready to retire for the night, but one more day and we'll arrive back at home, and that always has a sweet ring to it! God is good, and He has faithfully brought us this far and surprised us with many little blessings along the way. Because of the way He loves, I am challenged to always look for the good in others and in my day! This resolve brings me the balance I need in my life: balance between work and fun, serious and silly, giving and receiving.

So tomorrow I will continue on my way to the party.

On the Way to the Party
MAKING SCENTS

I've discovered my favourite drink of the season! Since you could never guess it, I'll tell you. It's rhubarb juice! I have my own method of making it and just recently came up with a way to enhance it. Last night after I had mixed the drinks and was sharing with a friend, she took a sip and commented on the delicious taste: "Point me to the beach!" How coincidental! I'd just been thinking, *This reminds me of the beach in Mexico.* I'm not kidding you. Not wanting to brag, but it really is delicious and refreshing and alcohol free!

I'm not here to promote my recipe for a rhubarb cocktail but rather to share a brief lesson that came to mind today. I was busily crushing the mint to be added to my juice when it struck me that the overpowering fragrance of the fresh mint was quickly filling my kitchen. I stopped what I was doing for a moment to revel in the pleasant scent and then realized that until I crushed the herb, there was no aroma. The sweetness poured out only after it was broken and crushed. It was there all along, but until tragedy (for the plant) struck, the beauty was sealed inside, unable to escape. I sighed. So like our lives!

In 2 Corinthians 2:15, Paul talks about our lives being the sweet aroma of Christ to God. What is in my life? What is in your life? When trouble hits and hard times come, the "crushing" begins. It is then that whatever is on the inside comes pouring out! Will it be impatience, hatred, unforgiveness, vile words, and downright nastiness? Or will the fragrance of unconditional love, the joy of the Lord, and words that build up and encourage permeate our space? Whatever we put in and nurture in the good times will pour out when circumstances get tough. The wise man that built his house on the rock didn't wait for the storm to come and somehow magically infuse strength; he built the strength into the house so that when the storm struck, the building didn't fall. It. Stood. Firm. And. Strong! On the other hand, the man who built his house on sand (not recommended as good foundation material) saw it crumble in the midst of a storm.

In this life, stuff gets thrown at us on a regular basis, but we get to choose what we build into our lives and what kind of scent we carry around with us. Is it the pleasant aroma that attracts others so that we can lead them to faith in Jesus Christ, or is it a stench that causes them to cross the street when they see us coming?

In this life, I want to be the one that draws others toward me, not *because* of me but because they sense the presence of Jesus in me. I want to walk in close proximity to everyone I'm bringing with me on the way to the party!

On the Way to the Party
SOMETIMES I HURT

Life is a potpourri of many things—things that bring tears that may fall gently or come in torrents. Maybe both within a two-minute span. Things that bring laughter, a tiny bubble that bursts out of you spontaneously or builds up to a dull roar that ends in a resounding belly laugh! Of course, there is always the stuff that puts you in the thoughtful zone or light-hearted realm, and let's not forget the gripping sadness that creeps into each life as well.

The past week has definitely dished out its share of that. Our family suffered the loss of a wonderful man, one who was hard working, caring, and loving. He always gave of himself to help anyone in need. I remember the times when I was blessed to be the recipient of his acts of kindness! When I was a new widow, he showed up to do a few tasks that took a physical strength I did not possess. His cheery, willing attitude made my day, week, and even my year!

As a long-standing member of my family (I don't remember a time when he wasn't married to my sister), he is very much missed, but I think of where he is at this moment and how he must be celebrating his arrival at this party I'm always writing about!

At a time like this, family tends to congregate to celebrate the life that was. I marvel at how just being in the presence of family members, many of whom I see only rarely, can infuse such strength and feelings of completeness and belonging into my soul. These are dear ones who can and have hurt us, but the miracle of forgiveness has created a turnaround; these are those that still have the power to hurt, but when the tough times come, we stick together. Those who make us cry also have the power to make us laugh until our sides ache, and as is typical in my family, turn back to tears in seconds!

I must remind us all at this time that family is not simply a result of society but rather a foundation designed by the creator God, and it's His plan to portray the relationship He desires to have with us. He made us to be His family. He loves us with all He's got, and He hurts when we hurt. He smiles when we smile, and I can even see Him holding His sides in doubled-up laughter as He beholds the innocent antics of His kids!

So how do we continue on when pain has suddenly shot its arrow into our lives? In my case, it worked to pull together as family and learn to appreciate and love each other again in spite of differences. This is where we encourage and lift each other up and maybe even celebrate our differences. In any case, I believe family is a good thing and a God thing, and I'm enjoying mine on the way to the party!

On the Way to the Party
FEED MY LAMBS

I have the weekly privilege of helping to distribute food out of a centre near my home. It would be an understatement to say I enjoy my involvement there. I would say that I have a passion for feeding people, whether it's good, nutritional fare or those yummy treats that are blacklisted by just about every diet plan out there! I am mesmerized by the sight of my friends and loved ones lifting fork or spoon to their mouth and actually enjoying the result.

So when I had an opportunity to tour the warehouses that supply our little hub with one of life's basics, I jumped at it. I was not disappointed; it seemed like acres of space were filled or waiting to be filled with goods that would lighten the load for many families in our city. It was here that I learned of the many programs run out of that centre, not only the one that supplies our needs.

For the first time I heard about the Food Box program. Boxes of nutritional foods are supplied to schools for the purpose of supplementing the children's lunches. Some of these kids may come to school with nothing, and others with very little and possibly nothing nutritional. Yes, I know we live alongside many that struggle daily to provide food for their families, and there are many little ones in my beautiful, blessed city that go hungry every day, yet I left there with a heart full of thanks to God for raising up faithful people who are willing to help fill the need, and eyes brimming with tears for those who find themselves perpetually in need. My tears are those of sadness for the ones that suffer as well as thanks for those that care, and joy that I can be one who does just a little, oh so little, to ease the burden.

There was a time in my life when I needed to visit a similar outreach and was accorded help, and my praise goes to God for providing for us in this way! Now it's time to give back. But I can't stop there. When Jesus told his apostle Peter to "*Feed my sheep*" (John 21:17b), I believe He was talking about bringing the bread of life, referring to Himself, to those around us. In my walk with my Lord God, I have found the deepest joy and purpose, one that leaves me satisfied with a relationship like no other. This is what I'm asked to bring to the world around me as well. As fulfilling as physical food is to the body, so walking and talking with Jesus is to soul and spirit!

So now as I head down the road every day, I'm reminded that there are many needs around me, and God is calling me to bring the answer, whether in the physical sense or the spiritual. Either way, I am feeding His lambs as I continue on my way to the party!

On the Way to the Party
A CRACKED VASE

I'm not sure exactly where it started, but it's quite possible it all began when, as a child, I was doing my regular weekly chore. At the age of seven this happened to be dusting furniture and assorted knick-knacks. One of these was a unique little vase with a crack that was really more of a piece that had broken out and was glued back in. For some reason I was fascinated by it. Then there was the ornamental blue jay that had lost the last inch of his tail. The broken tail end was splinted in with a splinter of wood, which when stuck into each broken spot, filled the hollow area just enough to attach the tail to the main part of the body to make it look just fine! I remember as a youngster being drawn to these items and wanting to know exactly how they had broken in the first place. I no longer remember the explanation, or if there even was one!

What I do remember is that to this day I love shopping at flea markets, yard sales, and bazaars. I'm drawn to items that have seen better days, and I enjoy bringing them home, cleaning them, and fixing them up. Making them beautiful and useful again has become a passion of mine. Nothing is too far gone; nothing is unworthy of a little extra time and TLC. I believe they call it re-purposing.

You probably know where I'm going with this. God made me in His image and breathed into me the breath of life. He designed me with a special purpose in mind, but somewhere along the way I developed a crack, a big one, that basically rendered me useless. Without intervention, I would have surely been trashed. Someone saw me in the back corner of the shelf, cowering under my coat of dust, ashamed of what I had become without a hope in the world.

This Someone picked me up, and He didn't flinch when I began to fall apart in His hands. Rather, His hands went to work, and He re-fashioned me into what I was always destined to be, a vessel that would bring honour to my creator. What gets me excited here is that He not only glues me back together, but He takes all the brokenness and makes of me a totally new creation:

Then I went down to the potter's house, and there he was, making something at the wheel. And the vessel that he made of clay was marred in the hand of the potter; so he made it again into another vessel, as it seemed good to the potter to make. (Jeremiah 18:3–4)

I have been made new, re-purposed, and given a job to do. Every day I try to remember that, but there are still days when those cracks show up, and my first response is to hide in the back of the shelf and let the dust and cobwebs fall. But NO—I recall the potter's loving effort to make me useful and beautiful. I no longer own myself; I am His, and His DNA is in me, which I believe is what keeps me aware of things that need a loving hand to be brought back to life again. More than that, I am keenly aware of people who need the hand of the Potter to lovingly remake them and bring back their beauty and usefulness! In fact, that is my purpose as I continue on my way to the party!

On the Way to the Party
TRADING UP

Some time ago, I heard the interesting, almost unbelievable, story of a young man who traded a paper clip for a pen. Of course, that was just the beginning; by the time the story ended, he had continued to trade up until he was the proud owner of a home, simply by trading in many varied items!

This brings to mind a time years ago when our then five-year-old daughter was quite eager to buy a piece of bubble gum from her older, wiser brother. Said treat had somehow miraculously survived a whole day after our weekly "treat night" the evening before! Older brother was smart enough to know that we would allow bartering to an extent without interference, but he dare not carry it too far. Finally, a price was agreed upon, and an excited little girl scampered happily up the stairs for her piggy bank.

"How like some adults," my husband said, "going after material possessions with all their energy, not minding the cost."

In this case I'm sure it was her brother who got the better end of the deal by trading up! In Revelation 3:20, we read, "*Here I am! I stand at the door and knock. If anyone hears my voice and opens the door, I will come in and eat with that person, and they with me*" (NIV). When I invited Jesus to come into my life, I served Him all I had, the very best. There's just one little problem with that. Outside of God, we're told that our righteous acts are like filthy rags (Isaiah 64:6). Jesus came to make us righteous through faith in Him. So when I laid out my best, all the pain, resentment, unforgiveness and sinful desire, He took part in all of it in what He accomplished on the cross of Calvary. Then He served me with forgiveness, peace, love, and the power and ability to live in victory! It seems that I am certainly the winner in this trade.

I invite you today to open the door and give your all to Jesus; He will then give His all to you, and you'll know what it means to really trade up. I look forward to swapping stories with you on the way to the party!

On the Way to the Party
JUST WAIT FOR THE GOOD STUFF

I have to say that patience has never been my strongest characteristic. However, as I have matured and gotten older, I believe I've been able to develop patience to the degree that now the struggle is less, definitely, than it used to be.

A very clear picture of what patience entails was presented to me about eight years ago. My granddaughter, about six at the time, took me up on the invitation for a ride to the nearest town. I had some business to complete there, and of course time with Grandma always included a "treat" break!

While rolling down the country highway toward the neighbouring town, we chatted about many things: Mommy, Daddy, school friends, brothers, and of course the kitten she hoped to have one day. At one point we were driving past a field covered in lovely yellow flowers. This caught her attention, and she asked me what kind they were. I answered that it was a whole field of canola. Then I went on to explain that when canola was ready for harvest, an oil was extracted from it, and that's the kind of oil we use to fry doughnuts in. I asked if she liked doughnuts, and she assured me she did, so we made a date to make doughnuts at Grandma's house when summer was over. With that in mind, we continued the drive to town, completed my task, and enjoyed our "coffee" break!

Shortly after we started back home, we again came across the lovely yellow field. Suddenly, an excited little-girl voice piped up and said, "Hey, Grandma, can we go pick some of the flowers and then make some doughnuts with them when we get home?"

I chuckled on the inside as I spoke to her very seriously, explaining how the flowers turn to seeds, and the oil is taken from the seed, and all this takes a lot of time. Maybe she didn't exactly understand, but I was confident she had the concept!

The Bible has a lot to say about patience. Here are a few verses for you to explore: 2 Chronicles 15:7; Galatians 6:9; Jeremiah 29:11; Hebrews 10:36; Psalm 40:1. These are only a few, and I'm sure you could come up with a lot more. All good things take time. Life and all that comes with it is a process. I'm reminded that when I was expecting my babies, I was very ready to give birth halfway through the pregnancy, but I knew the babies weren't ready at that point. How grateful I was to God for keeping them safely in their little "cocoon" in spite of my impatience. In each case, at the proper time I was delivered of a fully developed, healthy, adorable bundle of joy! Worth waiting for? You bet! More fun than a tub of doughnuts!

Do you suppose there will be doughnuts at the party feast? I'm not sure, but that feast itself is worth waiting for; don't miss it! In the meantime, I might munch on a doughnut or two on the way to the party!

On the Way to the Party
SUDDEN STORMS

A short time ago, I had the privilege of holding a book signing at a local book store. The afternoon was going along just fine; I had the pleasure of enjoying the company of my daughter, who was visiting from another province. We were sitting together chatting when I happened to look outside and se the trees bending practically all the way to the ground. The next thing I heard was the rattling of the roof. Since it wasn't Christmas Eve, I knew it couldn't be eight tiny reindeer! It had to be quite a storm out there.

Suddenly, without the telltale warning flickers, the entire interior of the building was plunged into darkness! Luckily my table was set up near the door, so what was left of the daylight found its way in to us. Without power, of course, the store was unable to operate; however, customers continued to browse where there was a bit of light.

Have you ever been in a place in your life where things seemed to be sailing along smoothly when suddenly and without warning you were blindsided by the "storm" of your life? Times like that can be devastating, knocking the wind out of your chest and leaving you gasping for air!

Nine years ago, I found myself in a similar situation. My husband of thirty-four years had just received his third cancer diagnosis, and for the first time since the initial diagnosis fourteen years earlier, he was actually ill and losing the good health he'd enjoyed for many years. We were at a good place in our lives. Recent empty nesters, we had plans and goals and were excited about the years to come. We lived near half of our grandchildren and enjoyed regular visits with them. We looked forward to watching them grow and become all that God intended them to be.

Then it hit! The blackness descended, and we nearly lost our balance as we struggled to get back on our feet again. It was here, and we began to understand, experientially, what the scripture says in Deuteronomy 33:27a: "*The eternal God is your refuge, and underneath are the everlasting arms*" (NIV), and in Psalm 30:5: "*Weeping may last through the night, but joy comes with the morning*" (NLT).

Yes, we were definitely in the night, as dark as it was; all we could do was apply what we knew of our loving God to our hearts and hang on to the hope that joy would come again. I can tell you now that joy did come—for me as I continued to lean hard on the everlasting arms that forever held me up, and for my husband when early one morning he slipped out of his pain-wracked body into everlasting joy and peace! Now he lives in perpetual celebration with the One, our Lord, who made it all possible.

One day we will all reach the end of our respective journeys, and there we will join in the celebration. Until then, storms may come, but as for me, I will hang on to God's promises all the way to the party!

On the Way to the Party
IT'S THE LITTLE THINGS

Have you ever noticed how little things can bring big smiles? It doesn't take a large production to bring a look of sheer delight to someone's face.

Years ago, I was operating a private daycare in my home. As a way of celebrating a week gone by and the weekend to come, I kept a drawer of tiny toys and goofy gadgets. Every Friday just before home time, each child got to choose one item to take home. This could be anything from a pencil to a small bouncy ball to cutesy little hair doo-dads. Such little things are of no real significance, yet how the kids looked forward to "prize day!" There always seemed to be that child who couldn't make a decision, so when the choice was finally made, she would mention from time to time in the week following which item she'd be picking next time. And, of course, there was usually another child who took delight in snatching it up if his turn came first!

Some years ago when I was going through a difficult personal struggle, I found my therapy in gardening. Nothing like getting my hands in the dirt to feel life's stresses ooze away and peace prevail! One such time when I was on my knees, I noticed a few clumps of what looked like miniscule little pansies peeking up at me shyly from the carpet of green grass. In surprise, I scanned the area to see where they had possibly escaped from. I had no such flowers in my flower beds, so I accepted that Creator God had simply put them there because I needed a little special love that day. I found out later that they're called johnny-jump-ups, and that's what they do. They pop up anywhere in the most unexpected places, a gift from my God just when I needed it!

A few days ago, my daughter surprised us with a visit from anther province. Both of us being nature buffs, we wanted to take a drive through Kananaskis Country. On the way I prayed, asking God to bring out at least one bear! I specifically asked to see a grizzly bear. In the almost thirteen years that I've lived in this part of the country, I've seen only one black bear in the wild, and never a grizzly.

We continued on the drive, filling our eyes and other senses with the beauty all around. Suddenly, we came upon the breath-taking scene of a huge grizzly bear sitting flat on his fanny and munching on the leaves of a small bush, just across the ditch from the highway. We were so close, I could see his skin ripple as he walked to another shrub and plopped down on his behind again and continued to enjoy his progressive supper!

I thanked God for answered prayer and was reminded of how He loves to surprise us with little "love gifts" in the course of our days. I've learned not to despise the little things, as they're goodies sent from the loving heart of my Father just to bring joy and sunshine into my life.

Psalm 127:3–5 talks about how children are a gift from God, and in other scriptures we read that good health is a gift or blessing from Him. The Bible contains many examples of the goodness and blessings of God that He gives to us freely.

I don't know about you, but I think I want to keep my eyes wide open and my heart alert to notice all the little sunbeams poured into my life as I journey on my way to the party!

On the Way to the Party
HOW BIG IS YOUR GOD?

She was only four years old and trying very hard to be a good little girl. It was never her intention to disobey (and anyway, no one had ever really told her not to do it). Now she could no longer escape that nagging little voice in her head that was telling her it was something she simply MUST do! After all, if she didn't at least try, how would she ever know if she could actually do it?

With great difficulty, she managed to climb up onto the ledge. It wasn't easy with her short little legs, but she had lived long enough to know that if she could just hoist one knee high enough to rest on the concrete edge, the rest of her would follow.

It felt dizzyingly wonderful to begin crawling along the edge of the cement cistern, which by the way was almost full of water for household use. The huge tank was right beside the basement staircase, and back then there weren't that many safety regulations, so in spite of her diminished size, it was rather easy to get onto the narrow ledge.

Suddenly, my mother's arms wrapped hard around me, and I was swung off the precarious perch in one swift movement! Then the scolding! Oh, I knew she had every right to land a good whuppin' on my mini backside, but having had my own children, I now understand that the relief was too great. Besides, she probably thought I'd learned my lesson when she described, in very graphic terms, what would have happened had I fallen in and no one was aware of what was happening! Not grasping the concept of not being able to swim, I'm sure it fell on deaf ears—ears that suddenly perked up when I heard her ask, "Who would have helped you if you had fallen in?"

Quick as a wink, I answered with "Paul Bunyan!" Well, of course. Being too young to attend school, I was all ears for the fascinating stories my older brothers brought home. And it seemed Paul was the hero of the times, so of course he would be quite capable of helping me, with his huge size and all! We went to church and I attended Sunday school and heard all the wonderful works of God and the miracles of Jesus, yet my first thought went to a mere fictional man who would be there to pull me out of trouble.

How often we fall into the trap, even as adults, of trusting our own human intelligence (or lack thereof) or leaning on our superb education or our ability to hold a good job and bring in a steady income. I pray that I will have learned by now that there are no true human heroes that can hold a candle to the goodness of a loving God. When you're in relationship with the God of the universe, you can expect Him to keep every promise He ever made. He will be there for you; His peace, protection and provision are yours *if* you are his child! Before you get out on that ledge, make sure you know on whom you can call. God is my hero now. Paul Bunyan? Not so much!

Please join me on the way to the party.

On the Way to the Party
PERSISTENCE PAYS

I cast frequent glances out of my kitchen window, waiting for the live show to begin. I had re-filled the bird feeder about four hours ago, and it usually took about that long for the bright eyed, bushy tailed species to discover the new snack! Then I saw him sneaking along the top rail of the fence. There he sat under the feeder, weighing his chances, and I could almost see the wheels in his tiny brain turning, measuring distance and calculating it against his size, weight, and reflexes. With one rapid, smooth movement he managed to get his front paws onto the edge of the tiny trough, and just as quickly his mini muzzle was buried in the delicious contents. This is where he got a little greedy! Wanting more and faster, he allowed his hind feet to leave the security of the fence rail. In mere seconds, his rear legs were flailing in mid-air, and eventually he was able to regain his equilibrium. But alas! He was now hanging on to the trough with all fours, but was upside down, his face nowhere near the tasty treat! As you can imagine, I was standing there at my kitchen sink in stitches!

As hilarious as it was to watch, there followed a sobering thought. I've seen many people do the same thing when going after something that was never meant for them in the first place— whether a relationship, a job/career, or just stuff. God has promised so many things to us, His children: peace, joy, comfort, His never-ending care and provision, health, and well being. These are all ours freely simply because, as His children, we're entitled to all that He has. Yet so many aren't happy pursuing what a loving God has prepared for them (Ephesians 2:10), so they go off the rails and give all they've got to get what they think they want. They end up getting hung up, upside down and clawing around for a foothold!

On the more positive side, I had to admire my fluffy friend's tenacity in going after something that he saw of value to himself. When we see a promise that God has given, let's go after it with everything in us, knowing that when all is said and done, we will receive the promise (Hebrews 10:35)!

Where do you see yourself in all this? Are you chasing after things that leave you feeling empty and unfulfilled? Or are you right now hanging on to a promise of God with confidence, waiting for the reward? I urge you to find and hang on to what God has promised! It truly is the only way to a full life.

As for me, I plan to hang on tight; I may arrive hanging upside down, but I'll be hanging on all the way to the party!

On the Way to the Party
OH BOY, OH BOY!

I'm not too ashamed to admit it; in fact, I'm proud of the fact that I love kids! They're just the most amazing, curious little creatures ever to walk this earth. In the past month we've been incredibly blessed to have a lot of our family visit us, four of which included children of various ages.

I learned a lot about myself during that time. For instance, I am old! One little guy asked me why my skin looked funny. I immediately thought, *Trick question!* So instead of committing myself I simply looked at him, wide-eyed, and replied, "I don't know. Why do you think it looks funny?"

The response came quickly. "Because you're old!"

If I was ever in doubt before, that certainly cleared things up!

Of the four families visiting with children, there were nine boys and two girls, all ranging in age from five to sixteen. They didn't all visit at the same time, but we did enjoy some overlap. It was sheer delight for me to sit back and just observe the distinct differences in gender reactions to their surroundings. The girls were a little more sensitive to others' feelings, and quieter and gentler in their responses, while still exhibiting an obvious spark and zest for life. The boys? What can I say?

Their exuberance in expressing aggression reaches all new heights when in the presence of cousins and adults other than parents. If you haven't yet caught on, I loved every minute of it!

Just a few days ago I was at a supper gathering where I struck up a conversation with a tiny girl at my table. She was probably six or seven years old and very anxious to go play in the playground next to us. She had been instructed to finish her meal first, however. In the course of our chatting back and forth, she paid me the highest compliment when she said, "I wish you were a kid so you could come and play in the playground with us." I assured her that I wished so as well. As the conversation took a different turn, she asked if I was a grandma, to which I replied that I was. Then she wanted to know how many grandchildren I had. Easy answer. "Eighteen." Then, "How old are they?" and "When are their birthdays?" By this time, I was laughing outright... not to make her feel bad, but I honestly can't remember all their birthdays. Since I inherited most of them recently, I'm still learning.

A few weeks ago, we had the privilege of hosting a young family from France for four days. She had been a foreign exchange student in our home in Manitoba twenty-two years ago. Now visiting with her husband and two boys, we re-established our relationship. On the drive to the airport on the morning of their departure, the youngest asked his father (in French) if people would understand him when they got back to Paris. His father promised they would, so he declared that he would then talk to everyone! So cute, yet my heart went out to the little guy, only six, who had spent three weeks in a country where no one understood him, and he did love to talk and tell stories about his day!

When Jesus walked this earth, He stood a young child in the midst of His very grown up disciples and boldly declared the worth of little ones. In fact, His pronouncement against any that would do them harm was harsh by any standards.

I'm afraid that in my lifetime of busyness, I haven't always lived by the words of Christ in my dealings with these precious little ones. My challenge to myself and all of you is that we remember their worth, not just eternal but here in this lifetime. Jesus made it clear that in order to enter the kingdom of Heaven, we need to become like children in their innocence, honesty, and purity of trust!

I can't wait to meet a few more of these wonderful little creatures on the way to the party!

On the Way to the Party
HIS HANDS ON MINE

Not long ago I was watching an interchange between a grandfather and his grandson; Grandpa was giving a basic lesson on how to use a mathematical geometry set. The young boy was struggling to handle the weapon-type compass. I remember the same struggle many years ago resulting in repeated self- stabbings! And you wonder why I struggle with math! Anyway, Grandpa patiently placed his giant-size paw over the slender hand of the boy and helped him maneuvre the instrument into doing what it was intended to do. The result was an intricate design of interesting proportions, with no first aid needed.

As I watched the lesson take form, I couldn't help but think, *This is exactly how it is with God and His children.* When we give ourselves over to His direction to fulfill His purpose for us, beautiful, interesting things happen! The closer we walk with Him, the less likely we are to be hurt and in desperate need of the healing only He can supply.

Picture yourself trying to accomplish a task that you know God has set before you. You're overwhelmed with feelings of inadequacy, and you just don't know how to get started. The accompanying fear is doing its best to cripple you and make you ineffective. This is *not* God's desire for you. His Word states that He will strengthen you to do all things (Philippians 4:13). That means all things He has asked of you!

I can remember many times when I didn't know where to begin in the task set before me; however, I knew that I knew that I knew that it wasn't my idea but God's. When I had that assurance, I could confidently ask Him to place His hand on my life and guide me through that difficult season. Emerging from the stretch of rapids my life had just come through, I could look back in amazement and see where I had grown personally, how the test had proven not how good a Christ-follower I was, but how awesomely faithful my God is. We are a team, and I will forever want to continue this path of being His hands and feet and mouth in this hurting world.

As I walk this path called *life*, I depend fully on His hand guiding me on the way to the party!

On the Way to the Party
HEADIN' HOME

I had just arrived back home after being away for almost two weeks. It was that time of year again when I would head east to visit family and friends. This is a trip I try to make about twice a year; it's difficult enough living two provinces away from daughters and grandchildren, and then there are my many siblings. Connecting with nieces, nephews, and even great nieces and their babies brought a few special surprises. One of the highlights was touching base with an old friend from elementary school days whom I'd not laid eyes on in about fifty-five years! We had dinner together and spent an hour and a half catching up. What a joy to share our lives, heartaches, and happiness. All the more to be thankful for and pray victory over.

As amazing as all the special people and visits are, nothing compares with the elation I feel each time I turn my car toward the west and head for home! You see, I'm quite the homebody at heart. As much as I love to go away and take a break, there's no better feeling than clicking my red shoes together and headin' home … figuratively speaking, of course.

As I drove, I gave way to my senses and allowed them to soak in everything just as it came. I noticed how the trees and bushes, which were a pale shade of green and barely kissed with touches of yellow on my trip east, had now graduated into golds and oranges. Even the leaves were letting go of their tenuous hold on the tree limbs and wafting down with the gentle breezes. As I drove into the day, the heat outside made it necessary to make use of my air conditioner. I found I quite enjoyed the contrast of heat on my left arm and shoulder caused by the sun's rays magnified by the window, even as I could feel the chill of the AC blasting its refreshing coolness onto my right arm.

In the rare moments between my favourite music blasting through the speakers and over the constant sound of highway driving, I could actually hear the sweet trill of birdsong through the closed windows of my car. At one point, I drove past a field under heavy activity and caught a whiff of harvest scent … just a bit of nose candy!

And, of course, I didn't miss the treat of wildlife—one lonely coyote trotting nonchalantly through the ditch alongside the highway. Then came the antelope, at least three small groupings in the field near the road. Yes, it was a lovely trip home!

I think of the road of life we're all travelling on, and for many of us the trip has its share of unpleasant surprises as well. Please know that you are not walking alone; in the times of loneliness and pain, Jesus wants to walk along as your companion. He desires to carry your burden of heavy sadness and cares, and He would love to share your sweet moments of joy with you as well!

I don't know how many more trips I'll be making across the country to see my family, but I do know that whether I drive away in my car or stay at home and live my life in the usual manner, I am loving life and headin' home on the way to the party!

On the Way to the Party
OH, THE PAIN!

It started as a faint, dull ache that just never went away; within days, it was like a steady drumbeat in the side of my head! Since I'd had a dental checkup, X-rays and all, just three months earlier, I never considered the possibility that it could be a tooth problem.

Having just returned from a couple of weeks away, I figured I could wait until after the weekend to see my dentist. But then I began losing pieces of an old filling; the time was now! I made the appointment and walked in with confidence. The dentist would simply take out the old filling and replace it with a new one … or at least, that's what I thought. Unfortunately, that was not how it played out.

After the initial freezing, the drilling began. Oh, how I detest that high-pitched whine! A few minutes into the procedure, however, I felt a distinct THUNK, like an earthquake in my head! The drilling stopped, and blessed quiet reigned as the dentist called for a camera. After taking a photo and showing me on the large screen where a crack had appeared clean through the base of my molar, she informed me there was no "fix" for this, and the tooth would need to come out. At least it was a molar, was my first thought. She then topped up the freezing and proceeded with the extraction. This too was no piece of cake. The end result was that she needed to add more freezing, since I could still feel the pain. Then came the saw, as the tooth needed to be cut into pieces in order to make it removable. By the time I left the office I was shaking, traumatized and longing for my cozy bed. And it wasn't entirely because of the bill I had just paid!

We all go through painful times. Sometimes we're tempted to try to live with the pain and trauma, thinking it's easier than dealing with the issues causing our problems. I want to tell you today that in the end it may very well be more difficult to get rid of the offending issue, but it will be worth it! Just like an infection needs to be lanced to allow the poison to drain out, or a bad tooth needs to be removed in order for life to become pain-free and pleasant again, so sin, hatred, or unforgiveness needs to be removed. That process can be difficult and bring its own kind of hurt; however, when it's over, true healing can begin without obstruction.

In the Bible, Jesus is referred to as the great physician (Mark 2:17; Mathew 9:12). If you read accounts of His life in the Gospels, you'll find Him healing people of many different illnesses and declaring their sins forgiven. He has no less power today; if you need healing in any area, call on Him. He's not limited in any way, but when our faith is engaged, He goes to work on our behalf!

My mouth is healing nicely, and I am so happy I made the choice to rid myself of that offence. I now can look forward to a pain-free ride on the way to the party!

On the Way to the Party
NO MORE FEAR

I was so afraid! Afraid of the unknown, afraid of what I was sure was just around the corner, afraid of everything that might happen, and afraid that nothing would happen. Sound confusing? I can't disclose at this time what was causing fear of such magnitude, but the fear was real enough. I found peace and strength only in the words of God found in 2 Timothy 1:7: "*For God has not given us the spirit of fear and timidity, but of power, love, and self discipline*" (NLT). This version interchanges the word "fear" with "timidity." I see someone facing a situation without confidence or assurance that he/she is not alone, but there is One much greater standing in for him. In any case, I find my peace and assurance in the fact that God Himself has given me the spirit of power, love, and a sound, disciplined mind.

So here's my next thought: a disciplined mind will purposely steer away from fear without basis. If there's a good reason for fear to rise up, there's still no good reason for fear to move in and control me. That's what a mind motivated by love and propelled by power does. It leads instead of standing timidly by and allowing fear to ride roughshod over us. I believe I will choose to walk away from fear and allow love and a disciplined mind to reign! Yes, I'm sure fear is on the prowl and will quite likely attack again, but between God and me, we've got this.

We used to sing a song to our young children that goes like this: "Ooky pooky, spooky fear, you have no right to be here. In Jesus' name get out of here, fear be gone, be gone, be gone. Fear be gone ... SCAT!"

If that's what it takes, that's what I'll be singing on the way to the party!

On the Way to the Party
FILL YOUR THANK TANK

It's that time of year again when we scratch our chins and strain our brains and try to come up with some unique things for which we can express our thanks. So why does it have to be unique or different? Our son had a standard line, or should I say word, when asked what he was thankful for: "turkey!"

What really inspires thankfulness in me is all the little things in my everyday; I am grateful to God for His daily provision. The words in Mathew 6:25–34 are so much more than pretty sounding poetry. They are a promise from my loving heavenly Father that all my needs are met because He cares for me. These daily needs go from basics like food and water, shelter, and clothing to all the peripherals that add beauty and warmth to my day: green trees that change colour with the seasons, green grass that feels cool and refreshing on my bare feet, and the many hues and sweet scents of flowers that fill me with gratitude for life itself.

The sensation of little arms around my neck in a loving hug, and a tiny hand exploring my face and poking an inquisitive little finger into my mouth, melts my heart with thanks to God, the creator of life and relationship!

The fragrant steam rising from my coffee mug as I sit with my legs curled up under me while I share a heart-to-heart time with a dear friend, daughter, or sister lights me up. This, all of it, is a litre of thanks to be poured into the tank. The more we pour in, the farther our lives will go, the more we can accomplish.

The Word of God assures us that our praise to Him moves His hand in our favour. In 2 Samuel 22, the psalmist gives praise and thanks to God and then goes on to describe all the works God has performed for him.

I've heard it said that what you focus on will be magnified in your life. If the focus is on negative things and circumstances, we invite more of them into our lives. If we centre our thoughts on positive things, the good in other people and happenings, we'll have more good things. We really can't see all the good around us without being reminded to give thanks for it.

I've shared a few of the things that move me to thankfulness, and this is a very short list. I could have included many more. Now it's up to you to create your own list. Have fun doing it! Recently I heard a line in a movie that grabbed my attention. It comes in the form of a question: "Are you happily grateful, or grumpily hateful?"

When I really stop and think about it, I believe I want my thank tank kept full so that I won't run any risks on the way to the party!

On the Way to the Party
GO AHEAD, TATTLE: MAKE MY DAY!

If you've ever raised or worked with children, you can identify with what I'm about to share. For over twenty-two years, I ran a private home daycare, and I have yet to discover something that brings a child more pleasure than the opportunity to "tattle" or tell on another's bad behaviour! If ever I was frustrated in my work, it had a lot to do with the nasty habit of tattling!

One year as summer was approaching, I realized that if I was to retain my sanity throughout the two months of vacation from school, I would have to come up with a very creative solution to this challenge. As I found myself doing on a regular basis, I began to pray for wisdom. The children in my home on any given day and *all* day would range from the age of one to eleven or twelve.

God, faithful as always, brought an idea to my mind that worked wonderfully for the next several years until I closed shop and retired from that line of work. One day near the end of June, I explained it to them as they sat and quietly munched their afternoon snack.

"Summer is coming," I said, "and I want you all to know that this year I'm going to allow all the tattling you would like without getting after you!" As expected, cheers went up all around the table. I went on to assure them that there was just one little catch: they could only tattle good things about each other, such as kind words spoken to another child, or deeds done by way of help or encouragement.

The reward would be "kid kash" that they could then exchange for a small gift or toy in a backyard pop up store set up at the end of July and again in August. The child who tattled and the one they told on would both receive the same amount of play money. The items for sale would have various price values, and the kids would choose based on how much kash they'd earned throughout the month.

The toddlers had no idea what was going on, but the older children were to tattle on them if they did something cute! I knew this would move the focus from looking for the negative to trying to see good, positive things in each other.

It worked like a charm, making the long summer days much more pleasant and problem free. I was amazed at how children are so quick to adapt from negative learned behaviour to a more positive focus with just a little encouragement.

In His Word, God has given His children exhortation to think about *"whatever is true, whatever is noble, whatever is right, whatever is pure, whatever is lovely, whatever is admirable… excellent or praiseworthy"* (Philippians 4:8, NIV). As we obey Him in this, we will find our focus turning from criticizing and judging to encouraging: *"Therefore encourage one another and build each other up, just as in fact you are doing"* (1 Thessalonians 5:11, NIV). The ending of that verse is my builder upper! The apostle Paul was watching his followers and acknowledged the fact that they were already doing the right thing.

My prayer for all of us is that we will take our focus off the negativity that surrounds us and look for the good in others. In so doing, we will encourage and provoke them to more good deeds!

So go ahead … tattle on me all you want. It will only make me a more positive servant of Jesus Christ, encouraging others I meet on the way to the party!

On the Way to the Party
TOO SORE TO SOAR

Years ago, my late husband and I received an anniversary gift from family; it was a special piece of furniture, an eagle statue with a glass top, ideal as an occasional table. Some time later, the top of it broke, so I recently had it repaired. It has now reclaimed its place of honour in the front entrance! Standing straight and tall, waiting to receive my keys, sunglasses, and other items, he has sort of become my own personal butler.

While I haven't personally studied the life habits of eagles, I have discovered some very interesting facts about this magnificent bird. It's been said that when an eagle begins to decline in strength and capability because of age and wear and tear, it will take action to reverse the negative effects on its body. The bird will hide itself in the clefts of rock high in the mountains. Here he will rejuvenate himself by pulling out old, damaged feathers and sharpening his beak by drawing it back and forth against a rock and allowing the friction to accomplish this task. He will also sharpen his talons in the same fashion. With a lot of feathers missing (you can imagine how he looks now), he stays put until new ones have grown in.

Now he's ready to rejoin life as he knew it. He will again soar above every storm that comes; when hungry, he can easily dive into the sea and catch a fish in his newly sharpened talons, tearing it to pieces with a renewed beak. In his twenty-to-thirty-year life span, he can again be effective and fulfill his purpose!

My question to you is: What do you do when life's storms get the best of you? Where do you go to renew yourself and bring new purpose back into your life? Jesus gave the invitation in Matthew 11:28: "*Come to me, all you who are weary and burdened, and I will give you rest*" (NIV). Right there, that's a great place to start!

Hundreds of years earlier, the prophet Isaiah penned these words: "*But those who hope in the Lord will renew their strength. They will soar on wings like eagles; they will run and not grow weary, they will walk and not be faint*" (Isaiah 40:31, NIV). Kind of looks like Isaiah spent some time observing this majestic creature himself!

Sometimes I feel my own purpose has grown dim and lost its sharpness. My ability to soar above is waning. How wonderful to know that in my own weariness I can go to a higher place and be renewed by my Higher Power, Jesus Christ. Now I'm ready to soar above life's storms and overcome the negative effects of all that life throws at me. No longer sore, I can now soar on the way to the party!

On the Way to the Party
WHAT'S YOUR HANDICAP?

Do you golf? I must be honest and say that I do not. However, I've heard the question above asked in relation to someone's golf game.

Many years ago when I was much younger and not so wise (sorry, avid golfers), I thought it would be fun to learn the game. So my husband and I went out one Sunday afternoon with friends. From the three of them, I actually learned a few things and made the mistake of thinking, *This is fun!* (Again, my apologies.)

About a week later, I convinced hubby to go golfing on our regular date night. We played the last hole in the dark, and after the final count, I realized with some shock that I had won! And yes, I do know that the lowest score is the winner. He never took me golfing again … hmmmm.

In the past three years, I've had two major surgeries, the last one being an attempt to repair and reconstruct my right foot after degeneration due to an old injury. Recently, as the lovely summer weather was waving goodbye and ushering in the cold, I began to experience ankle pain again. I cringe now to think how I used to laugh at older people who would attribute joint pain to the weather changes.

One day we decided to make a run to a large mall near us. My husband wisely suggested I make a visit to guest services and pick up a scooter to get around more comfortably. I was hesitant because I don't enjoy being viewed as being handicapped. In the end, I was happy I did! As I putted my way around the mall, I was intrigued by the various reactions from other shoppers.

Some gave me "the look" that said, "Why don't you just stay at home where you belong?" Others were a little more pitying, clearing a path for me as I went by. Then there were those, God bless them, who were helpful, not to the point of treating me like a helpless invalid, but by being sensitive to my needs. For instance, some helped me to get in close enough to the checkout counter, which was sometimes a challenge. Others kindly carried my latte to the table and made sure the chairs were moved so the scooter would fit.

God's Word has a lot to say about all human life, no matter the shape it comes in. Read Psalm 139 and see that you were on God's mind long before you were born. In fact, He wrote a book about you way back then! How about Matthew 6:26 and 10:31, where Jesus assures us that we are of infinite value and worth every bit of His care and attention? Jeremiah 29:11 states that God actually has and knows the plans He has for me, plans for hope and a future!

My challenge now is to see all my fellow humans as God does— significant, important, and of great value, made in His image. He makes no distinction, and He sees no handicap. He takes each one of us as we are and gently remolds and rebuilds us to fit His plan, if we allow Him to.

The closer I come to the end of my journey, the more aware I am of all God's creation. If I'm walking, pushing a walker, or riding a scooter, I will choose to be sensitive to all I share the road with on the way to the party.

On the Way to the Party
LET'S TALK ABOUT GOD STUFF!

Little five-year-old Sarah settled in at my kitchen table. As she waited for me to dish up her lunch, she piped up, "Auntie Ruby, can we talk about God stuff?" This little sweetheart had just arrived back from a morning in kindergarten and would be spending the afternoon in my home daycare. As was our daily custom, we would eat lunch immediately after her arrival, and as we ate and talked about all the important things that happen in the lives of pre-schoolers and kindergarteners, I would have worship music playing in the background.

Sarah loved a certain song performed by gospel artist Ray Boltz and would frequently belt out the words along with him. Out of that came many questions about God: Who is He? What is He like? What does He do? This particular day she just wanted to talk about "God stuff." My heart filled to the overflow point as she asked away, and I tried my best to answer in terms a five-year-old can understand.

Just sitting here remembering warms my heart all over again, and I pray that wherever this young adult lady is at this time, she will feel the presence of the God who caught her attention all those years ago; I pray that she will be drawn to Him in a depth of relationship that will truly make a difference in her life and home. Focusing on "God stuff" makes a difference no matter who you are or what your station in life!

I also remember the many times I've been drawn into a conversation, and instead of steering it toward the "good, lovely, of good report" stuff, I have wallowed in negativity and arguments. I'm not sure about you, but I leave that place feeling yucky and in desperate need of a spiritual shower!

I can't help but wonder how our lives would play out differently if we focused on being more thankful in our speech and speaking less about other people, government leaders, family, or drivers we share the road with. Since I will spend much less time on this earth than in Heaven for eternity *with* God, maybe I ought to focus a little more on including Him in my daily life. God is good, and He has great plans for me here. Therefore, I will choose to walk this path with love, compassion, and humility, talking about God stuff on the way to the party!

On the Way to the Party
GET READY

Remember when? Remember when you were a little younger than you are now, and you would attend those end-of-year school picnics? Everyone was classified into their appropriate age categories, and the race began with three basic commands: "Get ready, get set, GO!" I remember. I remember coming in last or near the end every time. I was not a fast runner, but I always persevered to the bitter end!

In the next few entries, I want to cover those three important directives. In this race we call life, it's easy to get encumbered with things that will slow us down, so let's "get ready." The Apostle Paul in his letter to the church at Philippi relates how he "strains" forward to reach the goal (Philippians 3:12–14). I don't suppose he did that while carrying a lot of extra baggage with him. The writer of Hebrews goes one step further and instructs us to *"throw off everything that hinders and the sin that so easily entangles"* (Hebrews 12:1, NIV).

Have you ever seen someone walking through the airport while wearing a backpack stuffed to the limits, balancing a bag under each arm, and carrying two large pieces of luggage, one in each hand? Oh, and I have yet to mention the blanket thrown over one shoulder and the computer bag over the other. That's entanglement! You'd never attempt that, but how many try getting through life while balancing hurts left over from childhood, which for some of us go back sixty years? These hurts have evolved into full-grown resentments, breeding bitterness and anger just below the surface. What about envy over something as small as the size of a friend's house, or a promotion at work? And we can't forget greed and all the issues it brings along, like the tendency to become a workaholic, or the temptation to cheat a little here and there in our finances. The author of the book of Hebrews encourages us to throw it all aside and run the race set before us, the life God has planned for us, the life He has prepared for us. Now we must get ready and allow God to prepare us for that life.

Just like no one in his right mind would attempt to run a race with all that baggage and "stuff" hanging on to him, we need to let it go and get ready to run the race and finish it! At the end of his life, Paul, claimed that he had *"fought the good fight … finished the race … and kept the faith"* (2 Timothy 4:7, NIV). Jesus Christ stands ready to take all those old burdens from you; He desires to give you freedom to run the race and win it! In 1 Peter 5:7, we're encouraged to cast all our care on Him, for He cares for us. I believe that's a good way to start getting ready to run the race on the way to the party.

On the Way to the Party
GET SET

We are ready, having relieved ourselves of all the "stuff" of life that has accumulated over the years. The pride, anger, resentment, envy, and all the old nasty hurts and habits have been left behind. In our wake, we may have left a few remnants as a reminder to keep on track and avoid the same pitfalls in the future.

For me, getting set is like planting my tomato plants in spring. As anxious as I am to observe new growth, I realize the need to be patient. It takes time for the plants to establish a root system whereby they will draw nourishment into the stalk, stems, and leaves. The goodness drawn from the soil will ensure the lovely, luscious fruit that I so love!

While growing up on a farm, I noted how my mother would put a hen to "set" in the springtime. With ten to twelve fertilized eggs under her, the hen would patiently sit and incubate those precious little fluffs of yellow until they pecked their way out of the egg shell prison they'd been in for exactly twenty-one days. That's the time it took to grow those cute little peepers out of nothing; that's the time it took to give birth to the "fruit."

In our lives, we get set by spending time in the Word of God. Reading, memorizing, and meditating on the Word are all ways of getting it deep into our spirits. There it can take root, or incubate, and in time grow the fruits of kindness, faithfulness, love, joy, patience, and wisdom. This isn't an exhaustive list, but rather an example of all the good that Father God wants to see displayed in our lives.

As we take in the nourishing Word of God, our spirit is fed and the roots go down deeper. As the roots spread out, we become more useful to the purpose of the Master. Meanwhile, during the deepening, or "getting set" process, we can't see what's happening. What's going on under the surface, in the dark, is finally revealed as new growth appears and fruit becomes available.

In Galatians 5:22–23, Paul lists the fruit of the Spirit of Christ: *"love, joy, peace, forbearance* [patience], *kindness, goodness, faithfulness, gentleness and self-control"* (NIV). These are all attributes that we grow into our lives as we allow our roots to go deep and get "set" in the soil of God's Word.

How would your life look if all the hindering weights were shed and the roots of your heart were encouraged to find their life-giving food in the things of God? How would my life look?

I am committed to this race called life, and it's a continual process of getting ready and letting go of things that slow me down. I'm challenged daily to allow myself to become more grounded in my Lord, Jesus Christ. Now I place my feet in the blocks and get set in the proper direction, focusing all my energy into running, heading in the right direction, and finishing the course. I wouldn't have it any other way as I continue on my way to the party!

On the Way to the Party
GROW!

Having gotten ready by ridding ourselves of excess baggage, with our hearts and minds set in the Word and ways of God, we're now ready to GO. When speaking about the life of a child of God, I believe that's synonymous with GROW. Growth begins when the roots spread far enough to support the plant and all its intentions.

As a member of God's created race, the plan for my life was laid out from the beginning of time, long before I was a gleam in my father's eye. According to Psalm 139, God knew all about me and had it all written down in a book. Ephesians 2:10 reminds us: "*For we are God's handiwork, created in Christ Jesus to do good works, which God prepared in advance for us to do*" (NIV). The growth, or fruit, in my life is revealed in my service to others. I recently read a beautiful phrase: "God doesn't waste a hurt." In 2 Corinthians 1:4 we read: "*And why does he do this? So that when others are troubled, needing our sympathy and encouragement, we can pass on to them this same help and comfort God has given us*" (TLB). Our purpose for growth is to bear fruit; in this way, we serve others.

When a new baby is born, he has all the muscles he'll ever need in life; yes, this helpless little bundle that moulds so softly and perfectly into your arms doesn't lack one single muscle. The only difference between him and his strapping big daddy is that Dad's muscles have been exercised and developed through constant use. Give the little guy a few years to grow and practise, and his muscles will match and possibly exceed his dad's.

As we live our lives, we'll encounter countless opportunities to serve others and bring hope and joy and peace into their lives. Part of this may mean sharing your own stories of struggles, failures, and downfalls. But don't stop there. Go on to share how God has used those difficult times to grow empathy and compassion in you, which you can in turn spill over into the lives of those you serve.

We have no idea who may be influenced by our honesty in word. Hurting people long to hear that there's an answer for their pain, and they want to hear it from someone who can openly and honestly admit to having challenges and being hurt, and then finding healing in Christ. Their ears are not so open to someone who, in their opinion, has it all together.

I have been there, struggling to balance all the pain, low self esteem, unforgiveness, anger, and self-pity—and not doing a good job of it! I also made the choice to let it all go and left it with Jesus, who gave me the strength to go on. I made the choice to plant my roots in the truths of God's Word and allow His love and life to fill me. I believe I am still growing in all He has prepared for me to do.

May I challenge you to grow with me as we continue this path on the way to the party?

On the Way to the Party
MAKE A DIFFERENCE

Have you ever met someone whose sole purpose in life seemed to be to impact those he met on a daily basis? At the beginning of this book, I mentioned that the title, *On the Way to the Party*, was inspired by my late husband, who enjoyed celebrating life—big occasions, small events, and pretty much everything in between. He would celebrate at the end of every day, thanking God for things I'm sure most of us would overlook.

It wasn't always like that. There was a time when he carried the weight of desperately needing approval from certain people in his life. The burden of low self esteem kept him down and dragging his tail feathers much too often. Then he decided to lay it all down on Jesus, the One who had already carried all that "stuff" for him. As he spent time with his Lord, a lot of those weaknesses melted away like snow on a warm April day!

Before my very eyes he began to grow into the man of faith he'd always admired in someone else. I do not downplay the need for professional help in some cases, but for him it was a matter of rooting himself in the Word of God, discovering his identity in Jesus Christ, growing in faith, and being a godly influence in his family, church, and community. Most everyone he met loved him, and if they didn't, he was okay with that. Sometimes I thought he was getting a little too okay with it! Because he was a prime example of one who exhibits the fruit of the Spirit of Christ (Galatians 5:22–23), everyone he met was impacted. He made a difference that counted.

We didn't know that his life would be cut short by cancer, but as one who shared his life, I saw the very real change that can happen when a person lets go of the old things that have gone before and chooses to "*press on toward the goal to win the prize for which God has called me heavenward in Christ Jesus*" (Philippians 3:14, NIV). I saw how he was able to build up the discouraged and speak hope and life into the most dismal of situations. He was always ready to leave a word of encouragement and a prayer with anyone facing a difficult time.

When it was his time to go, we could say, "He made a difference." He, like the great Apostle Paul, could say "*I have fought the good fight, I have finished the race, I have kept the faith*" (2 Timothy 4:7, NIV). Eight years ago, we had these words engraved on his headstone: "He made a difference." The prayers he prayed and the influence he left have become his legacy, and he is still making a difference. My prayer for myself and you, the reader, is that all who knew us in life will be able to say that when we are no longer here.

For now, I continue on my way, and I'll see you at the party!

About the Author

Ruby grew up on a farm in rural Manitoba, the youngest of thirteen children.

Being somewhat of an introvert, she always found herself looking below the surface to find meaning in life in order to make sense of circumstances, whether good or bad. Out of this came the potential to begin expressing her thoughts in writing.

In the busyness of marriage, raising four children, and running her home daycare for more than twenty-two years, there wasn't much time for writing. However, it was in those years, when surrounded by small children, teens, and later young adults, that most of her inspiration came together and many journal entries sprang to life.

After the passing of her first husband, Ruby decided to share their roller coaster ride through his illness as well as her grieving and healing process. In that book, God's faithfulness is exemplified over and over. It is her prayer that the goodness of a never-failing God will inspire and encourage the reader in this, her third published work.

With the advent of her second marriage, she added to her family eight more adult children and twelve more grandchildren, so life is richer than you can imagine, and the inspiration just continues to flow!

Ruby fills her spare time with involvement in her local church as well as in her community. She is available to speak and promote her books in church or community outreaches.

Please contact her through: email – rubywiebe52@gmail.com

Facebook: Ruby (Heppner) Wiebe

Blogsite: www.onthewaytotheparty.blogspot.ca

Other Books

BY RUBY (HEPPNER) WIEBE

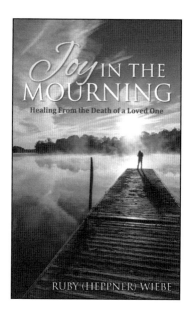

Joy in the Mourning

ISBN: 978-1-4866-1292-5
Retail: $11.99

You're looking forward to the best years of your life. Retirement isn't far away, the kids are grown up, and the grandchildren are coming along. Life is looking good!

Suddenly your dreams and plans take a nosedive and it's all you can do to breathe deeply and take one step at a time.

Is it possible to hold onto faith in the face of dire circumstances? Will you ever feel joy bubbling up inside you again? When a hope-filled solution is presented to you your spirits soar, only to come crashing down again when failure raises its ugly head.

You go to the only place where faith, hope, and joy can be restored. Even there you find you will need to make a choice: walk or wallow? Sing or sigh? Help or hurt? What will you choose?

Solomon Says

ISBN: 978-1-4866-1533-9
Retail: $11.99

King Solomon asked God for wisdom to live his life and lead his country, and much of what God showed him is captured in the book of Proverbs. Children love to learn and accomplish new things. This one-month devotional, presented in an appealing fashion and at their level, will teach children how to apply God's Word to their lives. With scriptures taken from the International Children's Bible, and thought-provoking questions posed after each reading, *Solomon Says* is an excellent resource for family and individual devotions.